W9-BZC-830

READER REVIEWS

"This is an outstanding book! I will definitely recommend it to our officers' families and it should be a requirement for police academies to distribute to wives of cadets and future officers. Allison Uribe does an outstanding job of relating everything an officer wife endures throughout the day in a manner that instills pride and understanding, especially for those who may struggle with the identity and role at times. She tackles difficult subjects and provides hope and certainty for our officers' families. Law enforcement families are essentially the foundation for any department and they need more resources like this to help protect and restore resiliency for our officers. Allison Uribe does just this in her daily devotional book."
-- *Brandi Burque Ph.D Police Psychologist*

"Too often people forget that law enforcement officers have a human side also. Allison Uribe reminds us of that human side from the perspective of a police officer's wife. Her heart and passion as she encourages wives to stand strong by seeking God first. A must for any LE spouse."
-Michael Armstrong
Deputy Sheriff (Reserve) & Missionary to Law
Enforcement

"The journey of being a wife on duty is filled with travails. Walk the path with Allison, as she will encourage those who kiss their officer goodbye and then hit their knees in prayer until he returns.
Use one, or mix and match as you desire. My words are your clay! I look forward to seeing the final version."
-Jim McNeff
Editor-in-Chief, Law Enforcement Today

"With the divorce rate being so high among police families, Cuffs and Coffee provides an encouraging faith walk for LEO wives at all levels of faith and years of service, along with tools to stand strong, respond to our officers with love and grace, and fulfill God's purpose for our families. This is not like other devotionals, it's specific to the concerns police families face. It's a hopeful journey into the tear-jerking reality of our lives, treasured moments, and shared fears. A perfect gift for a police wife!"
-Angela M. Riojas SAPD WIFE

CUFFS & COFFEE

Cuffs & Coffee

ALLISON P. URIBE

Copyright © 2017 Allison P. Uribe

All rights reserved.

ISBN-13: 978-1542371957

ISBN-10: 1542371953

DEDICATION

Dedicated to my officer, Joe. Your support moves me to reach beyond the stars. Your love moves me to write such words. Thank you for being my backup and loving me all these years. Without you and your faithfulness, dreams like this wouldn't happen. You are my dream and my goal.

ACKNOWLEDGMENTS

There is power in a praying wife on duty. For her mouth declares truth, professes her faith, speaks hope into her future, claims the impossible, and praises the one who holds her world in His mighty hands. As you journey through this 40 day devotional, it is important to remember the truth. The truth of God's word. While there is scripture throughout the pages, I encourage you to dig deeper into the background of the scriptures shared. Take the word of God and personalize it to your own life.

A wife on duty can't do it on her own. This calling is beyond our own ability. For even in the greatest distance, we know where our help comes from. Behind many police officers, is a brave spouse. May this devotional take you to a place of peace, clarity, and strength. It is important to set apart a special time of prayer and devotion each day. In this life filled with constant demands, schedules, and deadlines, let us remember that we serve a God who doesn't demand our time, but loves when we give Him our time. God doesn't expect us to have the day planned out with schedules, for He is the ultimate planner of prosperity. We are a work in progress wives on duty, so there are no deadlines, just us being His masterpiece in the making. Are you ready? Grab a cup of coffee and let your journey begin.

I AM A WOMAN. I AM A WIFE.

I am not just any wife. I am the wife of a police officer.
My identity is not based solely on those facts, but on how
my life is lived and how my marriage is unlike any other.
I am a wife who shares the sacrifice for your safety.
I am the one who celebrates holidays on a different day,
So yours will be safe.
I am the one who takes on a single parent role when duty
calls.
I am the one who knows strength at the news of a fallen
officer.
I am the one who maintains the peace in my home,
So my officer will know peace, instead of constant chaos
on the beat.
I wash blood off of his uniform, yet could never wash away
the stains on his heart.
And as my officer drives away, I am the one who remains.
I hold on to hope and strength, all while praying for his safe
return.
I am the one who knows my God and turns to Him in all I
face.

I AM A WOMAN BEHIND THE BADGE.

I AM A WIFE ON DUTY.

DAY 1
MR. AND MRS. 0460
*You are more than a police wife; you are a creation filled
with purpose*

"What does your husband do for a living?" There it is, a question not asked often, but when asked, there is a flutter in my heart. Some may not understand, but when I see his badge, I see what I took on as my own. Being married to a police officer connects my heart to him and all he stands for. While we may not bear the badge, we stand for what it signifies. So once my response is he is in law enforcement, I am then told, "Oh, so you are a police wife!" Yes, I am. I am a police wife, a mother, a daughter, a friend, a co-worker, or sister. I am more than just a police wife. I am a creation filled with purpose.

As we follow the Lord in our life, we are reminded God knows us and our officers by name. So even when others don't see the sacrifices made in our lives, the God of the universe does. When others see your officer as a badge number and label you as a police wife, God sees you for who you are and knows your destiny. God sees His beloved! Your identity is based on more than your status, but based on your unique identity and purpose in this world. We are not just Mr. and Mrs. Badge 0460, we are called by name and chosen to fulfill God's will in and outside of law enforcement. So while you are classified as a police wife in this world, your purpose and identity are in the kingdom of God. For your purpose goes beyond what any mind could conceive. You are redeemed and called by name. You are more!

"Fear not for I have redeemed you; I have called you by your name; you are mine,"

-Isaiah 43:1

Today's Prayer:

Lord,

Thank you for calling me by name and making me your own. Even when others don't see my officer for who he is, you do. Being a police wife is just one of the many blessings I am created for. While others see me as just a police wife, I love how you created me with purpose that exceeds such a role. Remind me often how I am yours and you are mine. Help me to show patience with others who don't understand this life of law enforcement. Help me to be a blessing in and outside of our law enforcement family.

Amen

Today's Reflections:

- Dont be scared to say your husband is in Law Enforcement

- God knows us by name

- others dont need to know of us, God knows.

THE LORD IS MY STRENGTH
AND MY SHIELD IN THIS
WIFE ON DUTY LIFE.

-Psalm 28:7

DAY 2
AMAZING VELCRO, HOW SWEET THE SOUND
Our lives are filled with many fond sounds.

Countless police families hear the sounds of a hero each day. We as wives hear Velcro, the buckling of their gun belt, the radio faded in the background, and the car drive away till we hear nothing. While many of us hear these sweet sounds and have made them a part of our everyday life, we often forget the sweet sound of amazing grace.

As our officers gear up for the beat each day, we hear familiar sounds that signify preparation for their daily battle on the beat. Far too often this normalcy in our homes turn to something amazing when the shift is over and the battle gear comes off. There is something about the sound of Velcro! It tells us they are home safe, and all is well. God's grace is something we should all come to hear, see, believe, and hold as our own. Grace allows us as wives on duty to do what we do each day. One of those duties is sharing the love of our life and his safety with our very own city and its' citizens. When the shift is over and we hear them rip apart the Velcro to rest, we can only thank God for his amazing grace in their safe return. The beauty about grace is that it is freely given to us each day. Only God knows the battles we face in life along with the battles our officer's face. God knows the battle and yet He is the victor of all! For when we fail or fall short, when our flesh gets weak, or worry creeps in for the safety of our officer, God's grace will be forever ours. For both the concerns of our heart and for our salvation.

But to each one of us grace is given as Christ apportioned it.

-Ephesians 4:7

Today's Prayer:

Lord,

Your grace is enough and far too often I forget that grace is mine. Grace is something I could never earn or understand, but yet you love me enough to give it so freely each day. In my everyday life, I thank you for it because I would be lost without it. As your creation of purpose, I couldn't live without it. As I cling to your grace when my officer leaves to patrol the beat, I hold onto it with hope for his safe return. Thank you for your amazing grace.

Amen.

Today's Reflections:

_____

_____

_____

_____

_____

_____

_____

_____

_____

_____

_____

_____

_____

_____

_____

_____

_____

_____

_____

_____

_____

_____

IT'S WHEN I WAKE IN THE MORNING LIGHT WITH A CUP OF COFFEE IN HAND, THAT GOD'S GENTLE WHISPER SAYS, "I WILL CUFF YOUR HAND IN MINE AND HOLD IT ALL THE DAYS OF YOUR LIFE."

DAY 3
THESE BOOTS ARE MADE FOR WALKING
Our walk is far more vital than our talk.

Duty boots. We see them in our closet, by our bed, and hear them as our officer zips them up for duty. They have walked into dark places, unfamiliar ground, and go where duty calls. From time to time I have touched his boots, and it reminds me that my officer walks into unsafe situations daily. So I pray. I pray that God would establish his every step and that his boots would be boots of peace. I pray that wherever he arrives, the kingdom of God arrives with him. As wives, we ultimately want our officer's boots to step back through our front door at the end of each shift. But while their boots are made for walking, we find that our walk in life is just as important. Our officers show up to roll call announcing their presence and nothing more. Why? Because their call is a walk and not made for talking. It is based off where they go and what they do. Our walk is far more vital than our talk.

We can mention so many plans, goals, and proclaim to be someone we are not, but what others will see, is what we do. God has called us to be doers of the word and to walk with Him daily. As we pray for God to establish our officer's steps, we equally need

God to establish ours. We should strive to walk in peace. We should trust that God will lead us to where we are called to. Many of us have heard the popular phrase, "actions speak louder than words." This phrase holds a lot of truth. As we allow ourselves to lead, let us trust that we are showing up and declaring to God each day, "I am here, I am ready, and I am trusting you to lead me to what I am called to do." Are you ready? Start walking!

In their hearts man plans their course, but the lord establishes their steps.
Proverbs 16:9

Today's Prayer:

Lord,

May I be a woman led by the spirit. Fine tune my ears so I may hear your direction and obey. As I go about my day, establish my steps and lead me to those I can help and show love to. When my officer patrols the beat, establish his every step so he may bring your peace into all situations. Together, lead us to what you have called us to and let us be a blessing. May our words be few and actions be an extension of you and all you are.

Amen

Today's Reflections:

_____

_____

_____

_____

_____

_____

_____

_____

_____

_____

_____

_____

_____

_____

_____

_____

_____

_____

_____

_____

_____

A WIFE ON DUTY WHO WAITS UPON THE LORD WILL RENEW HER STRENGTH.

-Isaiah 40:31

DAY 4
LATE BREAKING NEWS
When the news comes in, I will act and not react

News stories, you know the ones. The ones that bring out the worst in us and cause our thoughts to go "there". With every passing report our heart skips a beat. Emotions transpire taking us from shock, to fear, to anger, to grief, to exhaustion, and then pure numbness. We stand in the midst of loud opinions mixed with facts. Alone we cannot bring an immediate solution or even get peace. Perhaps we could avoid the news or remove ourselves from any form of social media, but it all comes down to our heart, and the heaviness laid upon it.

Guarding our heart is not something we often think of, and in this wife on duty life, we must. This will look and mean something different to each of us. There will always be news in our lives we love to hear and many we cringe at. In such circumstances, there is a hope with each passing news heard, that we would strive to act and not react. It can be a doctor's report, loss of a job, financial issues, family issues, or even an officer involved shooting or death. When we hear the news, it should be in that moment we remember to guard our heart, because everything will flow from it. Our response, our words, and our actions will be motivated by the things which flow from our heart. An attitude of action and not reaction should be a vital part of our many daily choices. In action we can make a difference, in our reaction we can't accomplish but a moment of emotion.

Above all else, guard your heart, for everything you do flows from it.

-Proverbs 4:23

Today's Prayer:

Lord,

With all the news I hear each day, help me to remember to act on the power of prayer and fight off any emotions that take my focus away from you. Show me how to guard my heart. Help me to put my full trust in you! Even when I feel like caving into my emotions, remind me you never fail. May my hope and faith in you flow from my heart into the world and circumstances that surround me. May my actions make a difference in all things!

Amen

Today's Reflections:

_____

_____

_____

_____

_____

_____

_____

_____

_____

_____

_____

_____

_____

_____

_____

_____

_____

_____

_____

_____

_____

AS HE GEARS UP....I PRAY UP

DAY 5
ABNORMALLY NORMAL
Days spent with no agenda are days well spent.

As I walked down the hall to peek in my daughter's room, I saw her coloring. Then, I found my two sons playing a game and carrying their own little conversation. Suddenly, the most beautiful sound filled the house, laughter. My officer was lounged on the couch relaxing while watching a television show with our German Shepherd next to him. I smiled so big both externally and internally. It hit me, things are normal right now. Everyone is fine. Everyone is at peace. Everybody is sharing in this normal moment. It couldn't have been more perfect and beautiful. We had no agenda, yet the normalcy we had was definitely a day well spent.

Normal for law enforcement families is rare. But when it happens it means, it's just "us", just you and your family. And when you share in those moments, something unique happens. It is as if time stands still and for a short while all the chaos of the world is not magnified, but the heart of your home is. In a world full of agenda and schedules, it is so important to remember that there is a time for everything. God himself has set a time for everything under the sun. Therefore as a wife and as a beautiful creation of purpose, rejoice and be glad in the days of normalcy. It is in the normal, mundane days where you find rest. Those moments are what we as wives on duty pray for and those are the days we long for. So when they happen, take notice and remember to spend it well! Time with your officer is one to be protected and prioritized, especially for your family unit. Not everyone will understand your priorities, but rest assured knowing God is your time holder.

There is a time for everything and a season for every activity under the heavens.

-Ecclesiastes 3:1

Today's Prayer:

Lord,

Thank you for the moments in my life when I can rest and know my family is safe. Thank you for the moments when I am blessed to witness my family enjoying the blessings of life. I pray that our family and I would experience moments where we can be in laughter and peace. Help us to not become so busy with agenda we forget the priority of family. Give me wisdom to use time wisely and to cherish it deeply.

Amen

Today's Reflections:

_____

_____

_____

_____

_____

_____

_____

_____

_____

_____

_____

_____

_____

_____

_____

_____

_____

_____

_____

_____

_____

*I AM NOT JUST A WIFE ON DUTY, I
AM HIS WIFE ON DUTY.
I FIGHT TO BE BRAVE.
EVEN WHILE FEAR IS A BATTLE IN
MY HEAD, I RISE ABOVE IT.
I NEVER EXPLAIN THIS WIFE ON
DUTY LIFE BECAUSE IT'S
UNEXPLAINABLE.
EACH DAY I AWAIT HIS ARRIVAL
WITH ANXIOUSNESS, AND PRAY THE
HARDEST PRAYERS.
HIS DUTY IS MY DUTY. HIS CALL, MY
DEVOTION.*

FEAR HAS NO PLACE IN MY WIFE ON DUTY LIFE!

-2 Timothy 1:7

DAY 6
THE VISITOR
Fear is temporary

There is always that one person we encounter who asks, "How do you do it? Do you ever fear for his safety?" As police wives we are all faced with fears for our officer's position. The questions people ask are almost monotonous, yet the curiosity captures them. With each question, it's as if our response is a yes or no followed by our concerns. While we worry, we cannot allow it to consume us. We couldn't thrive if we did. It is usually a temporary fear that visits from time to time. As we walk this journey, we ponder what it means to pray and to seek God's peace when fear visits our hearts and thoughts. Without realizing, each time we make it through. We stand strong and walk the line our officer fights so hard to keep. Fear is an emotion that can paralyze, yet with an unshakeable God we are reminded that we can face anything.

Even though we could never pinpoint the grace we receive to be married to an officer, we know this: When all is said and done, when the front door slams and his keys hit the counter, the sound of Velcro comforts us. We see their face and they see ours. In that moment, we know they did it! They made it. They are home and safe. The only thing left to do is thank God! Fear may visit from time to time in our lives. The fear we face can come in many forms and over a variety of situations. However, when we remember that our fear is temporary, it will bring hope to our fragile heart. In life we will face many challenges, be taken by surprise, and yet our emotions will surface with each one. God whispers in those moments that we are fighting a fight He has already won. In any circumstance we can trust all things will work together for our good, breaking down any fear that comes to visit.

"For God has not given us a spirit of fear, but of power, love, and sound mind."

-2 Timothy 1:7

Today's Prayer:

Lord,

When fear comes to visit, help me to run straight to you. Help me to rise above the fears I face. Give me strength, boldness, and courage. May my mouth declare that you have given me a spirit of joy, peace, and sound mind and not one of fear! Despite the challenges I face in life, may my thoughts and heart be certain I can overcome all things because of who you are in my life and all you do.

Amen

Today's Reflections:

_____

_____

_____

_____

_____

_____

_____

_____

_____

_____

_____

_____

_____

_____

_____

_____

_____

_____

_____

_____

THE HANDS OF A WIFE ON DUTY LOVE WITH GENTLENESS. THEY BUILD HER HOME IN PEACE AND ENCOURAGE HER OFFICER WITH WARMTH.

DAY 7
OFFICER DOWN
Grieve and transform

First it was one, then two, then four, and then a heartbreaking seven. The media announced the loss of seven police officers all within a week. This left countless people speechless and filled with numerous questions. There are never any words that could express comfort for any anguish that sweeps us when tragedy hits. But how were we to grieve this? What are we to do when faced with the tragedy of an officer down? Or any tragedy in life?

The answer is to grieve. The experience of loss can refresh our perspective in life, our marriages, or our walk as a wife on duty. When faced with walking such a dark valley, let us express our broken heart and pain to God. When we express that, He too can enter our grief. Even in a time of loss, we are promised a time to heal, a time to laugh, to cry, and definitely a time to rebuild what has been torn down. In such times we should rise and grieve, it's ok. But, do not grieve as the world does, grieve in hope and endurance. When we reflect on such tragedy such as the officers mentioned above, let us remember the lives lived. In those times, we must seek to continue what they started, by living in sacrifice for others, a way of life we should all strive to accomplish. An officer down moment is a moment in which we see an example of exceeding love, for there is no greater love than to lay down one's life for another. So, when life brings loss our way, we remember that grieving brings healing. In loss we will find a time to grieve and yet transform. We can transform into what we have seen displayed through the sacrifices made in the lives lost or what we gained in knowledge from any closed doors. Allow the grief in your life to transform you, mold you and move you forward. For even in death or loss, God can resurrect your heart.

Even though I walk through the darkest valley, I will fear no evil, for you are with me, your rod and your staff, they comfort me.

-Psalm 23:4

Today's Prayer:

Lord,

When I face the tragic news of an officer down, help me to rest in your peace. Thank you for walking this life with me and through the darkest valley's I face. In life when I experience loss, transform me and give me better understanding. Bless the families of our fallen and remind us that a life of sacrifice is a full expression of your love and faithfulness. Thank you for the comfort you bring to a world of hurt. Thank you for those who have given their life for another. Help me to live in such a way that will challenge others to transform, just as you have transformed me.

Amen

Today's Reflections:

_____

_____

_____

_____

_____

_____

_____

_____

_____

_____

_____

_____

_____

_____

_____

_____

_____

_____

_____

_____

_____

_____

_____

A WIFE ON DUTY
KEEPS WATCH OVER
EVERYTHING
IN HER HOUSEHOLD, HER
HEAVENLY SUBSTATION....

-Proverbs 31:27

DAY 8
A PRAYING WIFE ON DUTY
Praying is a successful tool in our marriage.

As we reflect on the challenges, we have faced and continue to face as wives on duty, one can almost wonder about society's concept of success in a law enforcement marriage. Knowing the statistics and marital struggle in this profession, would that affect our thinking about what it means to achieve success in our own marriages? I recall a time when I listened to a few women discuss how they keep their marriages stable. Each of them had their own solution, customs, and ways. Many of these solutions involved a weekly date night, spending an hour talking each day, putting the kids to sleep early for time alone, and other ideas. Finally, one woman said, "I think the key to a great marriage is prayer." Each marriage and individual person is different. A successful marriage is one that involves learning and a lot of forgiveness. The woman who mentioned prayer, prayed with hope. She sought to get great attributes that would not just bless her officer, but herself. She understood that success would require seeking the Lord and His will. The battle is on for our marriages today. As wives on duty we face unique battles, such as the high stress of our officer's work, constant changing shifts, long work days, and the toll the job takes upon our loved ones. We must decide if we will allow these battles to defeat us or if we will face them head on, emerging victoriously. We must choose success! We remember that we are all imperfect as are our marriages. By relying on God and seeking him each day in prayer, we can seek to achieve our personal level of success. In leaving our trust issues with God we express hope. Hope is defined as "to expect with confidence" and we express this when we pray. Prayer is one tool that will guide us to be successful in life! Prayer is a conversation worth having with a God who holds all power and gives us the confidence we need to expect with great expectation.

*Then you will call on me and come and pray to me,
and I will listen to you.*

-Jeremiah
29:12

Today's Prayer:

Lord,

Thank you for the gift of prayer. Thank you for
listening as I give you my concerns. I know my
officer and I will fall short of your glory, but cover
us in your grace and help us to be successful. Bless
our marriage and help us to be an extension of your
love to one another. In all things we face, let prayer
be our solution and tool. Give me the confidence I
need, to know when I come before you, you will
answer.

Amen

Today's Reflections:

A PRAYING WIFE ON DUTY EXPECTS WITH CONFIDENCE!

DAY 9
I DO
"I do" is an everyday choice.

A fellow wife on duty once said she invited God to her wedding by getting married in the church, but she didn't invite him into her marriage. How often do we fail to include God in our marriage each day? From the moment we said "I do," we made a vow to our spouse and they to us. We understand that each vow cannot be sharpened and fulfilled without failure. It's not about having a perfect marriage, home, or life, but it's about growing together and learning from each other. This commitment will require you to say, "I do" each day. The word "do" means, "to bring to pass, to commit, to perform." With a life full of time consumption, we will fail each other and the "I do" commitment can be a challenge.

In marriage, love brings about expression and the desire to fulfill an unselfish task. Love is an action word! The words "I do" can mean many things such as choosing to forgive, choosing to understand, choosing to love unconditionally, or choosing to listen. When you said your vows, you chose, a decision to carry out your love. In life we will have choices to make. We will be given the option to do things while choosing to not do others. The important factor is not to just do good things, but to do God's thing. When we invite God into our marriage, work, relationships, and circumstances, we find that we will do all God desires us to do. It will no longer be about works, but about fulfilling purpose and committing ourselves to doing God's work no matter what it may look like. So in a life of uncertainty and failures, we can trust that when we invite God in. He will enter and do what we could not.

Whatever you do, work whole heartedly, as for the lord and not men, knowing from the lord you will receive the inheritance as your reward.

-Colossians 3:23-24

Today's Prayer:

Lord,

Forgive me for not always including you in every detail of my life. As I go about each day, guide me to do all you need me to. Let your agenda be my agenda, may your will become my purpose. In everything I do, let it glorify you. Help me to say, "I do" each day to what you have entrusted me with. May I fulfill my purpose and run the race well.

Amen

Today's Reflections:

WHETHER YOU TURN TO THE RIGHT OR LEFT, YOUR EARS WILL HEAR A VOICE BEHIND YOU, SAYING, "THIS IS THE WAY, WALK IN IT."
-Isaiah 30:21

DAY 10
DISPATCH PLEASE
What we communicate is found in our actions.

Communication comes in many forms. We communicate with the words we speak or write, but we also speak through actions. What is it about our actions that leave an everlasting impression? The word communication is derived from the Latin word "communis" which means to share. Therefore, when we communicate with words or actions to our officer or others, we are sharing. Communication can be one of the most difficult aspects to master. How can we best communicate with those within our daily reach? It would mean putting our life into action and responding in a way that expresses godly love!

Action communication can achieve much more because it reaches the heart. Just as a dispatcher knows the location and hears the need, we too can gain insight of knowing all needed for any situation. This knowledge will bring out our best possible love and action to any situation. How? By asking the Holy Spirit. When asking for Holy Spirit guidance, it is like asking the dispatcher to help us navigate. But even in the word we find an answer and description of what it means to communicate love.

We must seek God's wisdom on how the love we show to those around us, reflect God's love. In the scriptures we find love's definition in 1 Corinthians 13:4-7. After reading this verse many of us would agree that the love we communicate to our officer or others falls short. The love we express may never line up to such a degree, but with God, we can strive to come as close as possible. Learning to love as Christ did is one of the most amazing feelings one can experience. Love brings about expression and the desire to fulfill an unselfish task. The most beautiful expression of love recorded in history is that of the cross with our Savior stretching out his arms and dying for us all. The beauty of his unselfish love cannot be compared. No one can understand or comprehend its power. The cross is God's communication to you that His love has no boundaries and just think, He did it without words.

"Love is patient, love is kind. It does not envy, it does not boast, it is not proud. It does not dishonor others, it is not self-seeking, and it is not easily angered. It keeps no record of wrongs. Love does not delight in evil but rejoices with the truth. It always protects, always trusts, always hopes, and always perseveres."

-(1 Corinthians 13:4-7).

Today's Prayer:

Lord,

I pray that the Holy Spirit would be my dispatch in guidance. For loving others, give me wisdom and insight to love according to their need, and yet love according to your will and purpose. May the Holy Spirit also be the ultimate dispatcher in my officer's life. Thank you for your expression of love for me and this world. Let me be a vessel you communicate through and may it be fruitful.

Amen

Today's Reflections:

_____

_____

_____

_____

_____

_____

_____

_____

_____

_____

_____

_____

_____

_____

_____

_____

_____

_____

_____

_____

_____

AND YET I CRY....

The danger has always been there, there was never any doubt. But with the way things are going I wish he could get out. He took an oath of Honor and I followed behind. I never knew the severity of walking this thin blue line. And yet as I walk it each day beside him in faith, I see the oath taken and I stare it in the face. And yet I cry with tears of sadness, for the oath is far too great. To ask him to leave this, too much would be at stake. For this world needs a hero, someone to stand up for what's right. Because he believes in the oath, I will choose to stand with him and fight. For no one could do what he is called to each day, and yet I cry when all I can do is pray. Prayer is the one thing I whisper so strong. Beside the badge is where I belong.

A WIFE ON DUTY WALKS IN STRENGTH WITHOUT FEAR OF THE FUTURE.
FOR HER FUTURE IS HELD IN THE PALM OF A MIGHTY HAND...

DAY 11
PEACE OFFICER
Peace is a portrait waiting to be created.

With the many stresses our officers carry, including our own, peace is something hard to maintain. We become consumed in our lives and with added stress each day, maintaining peace can be such a challenge. With law enforcement being a part of our life, it is best to maintain peace not only because of the chaos our officer's face, but life as it unfolds for us. Peace is a portrait waiting to be created not just by God's hand, but by your hand extending His. The joy in creating a peaceful atmosphere is one joy of giving we can't afford to ignore.

While our officer reports to duty at their substation, our home and ultimately our love for them, is a heavenly substation they will never have to report to, but only come home to. If we take notice, we see that our attitude and outlook sets the atmosphere all around us. Peace can transpire from within when we get in step with God and allow Him to be the commander of our heavenly substation or daily walk. Peace seeking will require to lie down our burdens and to trust God will be the calm in our daily storms. Our officers bring their stress home whether we see it or not, it can easily cause stress not only in us, but in those who surround us. Many officers do not care to discuss their line of work. Many will downsize all they have seen as it is easier to not face such darkness head on. The same is in us as wives and as individuals. There are times you may have no peace because you are broken into pieces. There are dark things you may have faced in life that is difficult to discuss. In such times it will be piece by piece you can find the peace only God can give. It will be a self-choice that will give you the courage to be the peace officer of your days and seek your God when it feels as if your world is caving in.

"And the peace of God, which transcends all understanding, will guard your hearts and your minds in Christ Jesus."

-(Philippians 4:7)

Today's Prayer:

Lord,

Your peace is indescribable and so freely given when asked for. Give me a peace that surpasses all understanding in this life. Extend that same peace to my officer as he goes about the beat. Give me the knowledge needed to bring peace into our home, into our family, and wherever I step foot. Create in me a clean and peaceful heart so I will be a light of peace in this world. Help me to choose peace each day and not allow the enemy to come in and steal it from me or my family.

Amen

Today's Reflections:

_____

_____

_____

_____

_____

_____

_____

_____

_____

_____

_____

_____

_____

_____

_____

_____

_____

_____

_____

_____

_____

_____

A WIFE ON DUTY TRUSTS IN THE LORD AND LEANS NOT ON HER OWN UNDERSTANDING

-Proverbs 3:5-6

DAY 12
SHARING YOUR HEART
When your officer serves, you serve with him.

Our law enforcement officers save many from distress and are the key to keeping our cities safe. Without realizing, the safety they provide is being shared by the ones who cherish them the most, and that's you! Although we as wives on duty are not officially sworn into the department, we are sworn in by the love we share and have promised. Your support and encouragement in their call to duty is shown when you allow your officer to walk out of the door each day. Even though there are times you find yourself unsure of their safe return, you still share your heart, for the heart of your city. It can feel like a lonely road, but this is where God promises he will never leave or forsake you.

In life we will sacrifice much and specifically as the wife of a law enforcement officer. In each instance where we feel alone or as if we are behind and not beside the badge, you know that when your officer serves, you serve with him. This call to duty is not just for one, but for two. One without the other would fall apart. Sharing your officer speaks volumes about living a life of giving. In life we will be expected to give in numerous capacities. It could be a giving of your time, energy, finances, or even a listening ear, but not a single act of giving goes unnoticed by God. Each time you give or share, you are sharing your heart with those who receive. As you give, you are planting seeds of love and goodness that will later manifest and bring forth blessings in your life. Let us seek God in all we do so that our hearts will be a service to those around us and to those we cherish most. May the service of our heart know no boundaries and carry into the city our officer serves and protects.

"Whoever serves me must follow me; and where I am, my servant also will be. My father will honor the one who serves me."

- (John 12:26)

Today's Prayer:

Heavenly Father,

What a gift to have a heart of service. Thank you as I witness it daily in my officer. Use me each day to be a giver of love and one who sacrifices for the sake of others. May my heart be an extension of your heart and establish my feet to follow you all the days of my life. May my life honor you, may my officer honor you, and may our city feel your love through us both.

Amen

Today's Reflections:

_____

_____

_____

_____

_____

_____

_____

_____

_____

_____

_____

_____

_____

_____

_____

_____

_____

_____

_____

_____

_____

_____

_____

YOU ARE MORE THAN A WIFE ON DUTY. YOU ARE THEE DAUGHTER OF A KING. YOU WERE BORN FOR GREAT AND MIGHTY THINGS!

DAY 13
HANDS BEHIND YOUR BACK
God can take captive any shame in your heart.

Every day we are surrounded by people with different stories, hurts, and pasts. The internal hurt we carry, many don't see, but God does. There are stories of abuse, stories of regret, some stories of loss, but many of them masked and hidden into the deepest corner of our hearts. A simple, "How are you" has been an expected question to be followed by an expected answer of, "I'm good." How often we claim to be okay when inside we are hurting or feel shame.

Many of our officers come home after a day on the beat having witnessed what may couldn't bear to see. While people come home with a physical briefcase, officers hold an internal briefcase in their hearts and thoughts. There are many officers able to leave work behind, but there is also a vast majority not intending to take it home, who do so. Like our officers, we too have carried our life struggles and hidden it in the briefcase of our heart. God says, "I see the deepest corners of your heart and I take captive each one." Because God has created you to be free and of free will, with each passing thought,

ALLISON P. URIBE

pain, or trauma, turn to God and allow him to consume it all. Just as an officer goes out in search, so God will search your heart. Just as an officer cuffs and detains, God will cuff your heart ever so close to His. As each officer follows the commands of a dispatcher, follow out the direction of the Lord and in that find the discernment to know what He asks of you. Release the pain, release those deepest things into His care, for though he is invisible, God is very much alive and living in you, including those dark places no one will ever see. While God's hope for you and your officer is to not carry burdens home, He wants you to take those burdens home with Him and let Him handle them. When others ask how you are, be confident as God's child to answer with truthfulness, but yet with hope in your heart. Shame is not a part of the deal, for there is no condemnation for those who love Him. You were never meant to walk with your hands behind your back. You were called to live in freedom.

There is no condemnation for those who are in Christ Jesus.

- (Romans 8:1)

Today's Prayer:

Lord,

There has been shame in my heart at many times in my life. At your feet is where I long to be so I can feel the freedom you have given me and this world. Thank you for allowing us to walk in your freedom. Thank you for not condemning us but sanctifying us through the blood of the cross. Please take the shame that lingers in my heart and replace it with joy in that area. Give me confidence to rest in your love. Give me joy as I discover your truth, so I can be set free!

Amen

Today's Reflections:

_____

_____

_____

_____

_____

_____

_____

_____

_____

_____

_____

_____

_____

_____

_____

_____

_____

_____

_____

_____

_____

SWEET WIFE ON DUTY, GOD WILL NEVER LEAVE YOU OR FORSAKE YOU...
-Hebrews 13:5

DAY 14
TEARS OF THE HEART
The tears of the heart pour when there is nothing left within.

It was after midnight when he walked through the door. The pounding of the rain and slamming of the door echoed in the house. Approaching him, it was obvious he was drenched with the night he had on the beat. As he looked over with dismay, the words came out of his eyes and not his mouth. Pure silence. Latex gloves would do it for now as blood covered across the chest of his uniform. Who dare ask what happened when one could only imagine. I grabbed his uniform and lay it in the washer understanding I could never wash away the memory of a tragedy.

Many of us are drenched with the unimaginable or will be surrounded by others drenched in pain. While we see the physical tears, we must remember many are walking around with tears pouring from their heart. You can only assume the pain or even offer a temporary relief, but what good is it when we can't bring them a permanent relief in Jesus Christ? To live a life of giving is to live a life of blessing. One could relate giving to offering money when in fact giving has no boundaries. Has God called you to give someone a listening ear, perhaps be a shoulder for someone to cry on, now is the time to ask Him. Each day we should seek the Lord in how He would desire us to give. It will mean allowing God's agenda to become our own. We as wives of officers will have times when we need to be the helper God has called us to be. When words are unnecessary, we move toward what has been engrained in our human nature since the moment we were born, to show compassion. Living a life of compassion will require us to not set limits and expand our way of thinking each day to reach all we come in contact with. When we discover a person drenched with the chaos of the day, including ourselves, we must remember how God drenches us with his love. Far too often we allow ourselves to drown in our sorrows and troubles. Now is the time to drench our sorrows with the power of God's miraculous touch. Tears of the heart may flow, but nothing can stop God from wiping each one.

Weeping may endure for the night but joy comes in the morning.

-Psalm 30:5

Today's Prayer:

Lord,

When tears of the heart flow in me or those around me, help me to extend compassion. Take compassion to a whole new level in my life. Forgive me if I have ignored someone hurting or didn't take time to listen. Lead me to those hurting around me so I can be a light in their darkness. Shine through me each day and let them see you before they see me. Bring joy to those I love each morning. Bring joy to my heart each day and may it overflow into the lives of others.

Amen

Today's Reflections:

DAY 15
UNDERCOVER
All that is covered and hidden must come to light.

We are fed information daily. Much of the information we receive is unnecessary for safe keeping, but sometimes we are given information that is vital and important in keeping undercover, secret. In marriage we are held to a level of no secrecy and pure transparency. There is a trust established as husband and wife. But what would you do if you were given information involving your partner, your officer? Such an incident occurred one day where I battled whether I should share this knowledge of information with my spouse I had overheard. In my heart, I knew it not to be true and there must have been a misunderstanding. I knew if I had exposed and uncovered what was hidden, light and an answer would be found. Holding such a secret caused me to be silent and behave in a way that even my officer noticed. There was an internal thought battle and out of nowhere my mouth spoke, "THIS IS THE ENEMY." The enemy had messed with my thoughts and I allowed him to by withholding. I shared with my officer what I had discovered. Laughter came from him. I was puzzled, what was he laughing at? I discovered there was a huge misunderstanding and before I knew it, we were both laughing. What was hidden was now in light and it brought peace and a definite burden off of me.

There are times we will be given information and told not to share with anyone, including our spouse. Trust can be violated in such circumstances depending on the situation. Only God can give you the wisdom on what needs to be withheld and what needs to be shared. God's word says what is concealed will be brought out into the open and there is nothing hidden that will not be disclosed. There should be a trust in marriage that even the most hidden of secrets are revealed. Transparency is beautiful and can bring a deeper level of intimacy within your marriage. In the beginning, Adam and Eve were naked in the garden showing us that marriage was made to be filled with transparency and knowing all of one another. This is also the case with our heavenly father, God wants to know all there is to know about you. He knows everything about you, but He wants to hear your voice and know all the things that the world will never see. All the undercover things in your heart, life, and marriage can be brought to the light of Jesus Christ. Only God can expose and cover in grace.

For there is nothing hidden that will not be disclosed, and nothing concealed that will not be known or brought out into the open.

- Luke 8:17

Today's Prayer:

Lord,

Please give me the courage to expose what it is hidden. Help me to be transparent with my officer. Build up the trust in our marriage each day. Give me wisdom when faced with secrecy. As I go about my day speak to my heart about the things undercover in my life.

Amen

Today's Reflections:

_____

_____

_____

_____

_____

_____

_____

_____

_____

_____

_____

_____

_____

_____

_____

_____

_____

_____

_____

_____

_____

_____

_____

HE IS MORE THAN JUST A NUMBER ON A BADGE. HE HAS A NAME, HE HAS A FAMILY, AND HAS HIS OWN DREAMS AND ASPIRATIONS. HE FIGHTS BATTLES NO OTHER DARE APPROACH. HE HAS A GOAL TO COME HOME SAFELY EACH DAY. HE IS LOVED. HE IS HONORED. HE IS RESPECTED. AND THE BEST PART, HE IS MINE AND I AM HIS.

HE WILL LEAD
YOU BESIDE STILL WATERS
AND RESTORE YOUR SOUL...

-Psalm 23:3

DAY 16
COME OUT OF HIDING

While we may hide from the world, we need not hide from the Lord.

"The delivery guys are almost here honey, don't forget to take down our picture in uniform and put away anything police related from the shelf." It happened just like that. I could see concern in his eyes, frustration, and did I see fear in his eyes at the news of yet another officer involved shooting? Maybe, do I blame him? As I removed all police décor, I could sense God reminding my heart that if the world has left us or chosen to come against us, God will never leave or abandon us. Questions filled my mind as I stepped back and thought, "Has it really come to all this? Are we hiding now?" Many of us have felt the need to hide whether it be on social media, from sporting our latest police shirts or bumper stickers, or even concealing our officer's occupation. But there is always a gentle reminder we have a God who is real no matter how we feel.

Even in our fears and concerns, God is real. Now more than ever, we need to discern what is fear and wisdom in our lives. Struggling with fear can be difficult, but there must be a fight to ensure it does not enter our home. You can be the difference that sets the tone in any home situation. Your officer, children, and loved ones are watching. The truth will transform you because the real God you know will never leave your side. God is right there, right beside you. So, while hiding may feel like an answer, you need not hide because it is God himself who protects you beyond what your mind can comprehend. He has ordered the number of your days, no one can change that. We need to distinguish the difference between fear and wisdom, not just in concealing our law enforcement status, but any status we hold in life. When possible, choose wisdom. As police wives, we cannot live in fear and God's perfect love casts out all fear. It will mean staying ever so close to God in prayer. It is time to come out of hiding because we are safe in the Lord's keeping. We can conceal and hide many things from the world, but it is the God of angel armies who goes before, behind, and beside you. It is God who pre- approved you!

For he will command his angels concerning you to guard you in all your ways.

- Psalm 91:11

Today's Prayer:

Lord,

When I face fear of who we are, remind me it is you who commands your angels to guard us. Give me discernment to distinguish wisdom and fear and know the difference. It feels safest to hide from the world, but I know you didn't create me to live in fear and in hiding. Give my officer and I peace as we walk this thin blue line. Give me confidence in who you have created me to be.

Amen

Today's Reflections:

_____

_____

_____

_____

_____

_____

_____

_____

_____

_____

_____

_____

_____

_____

_____

_____

_____

_____

_____

_____

_____

IT IS GOD WHO KEEPS MY OFFICER. HE IS HIS BULLET PROOF VEST, HIS LIGHT IN THE DARK, HIS SHIELD FROM THE STORM, AND HIS BACKUP!

DAY 17
BURNOUT

Even in exhaustion those who trust in the lord will have renewed strength.

The alarm clock went off and he rose out of bed. I could see he wanted ten more minutes of sleep. He geared up, kissed me goodbye, and patrolled the beat like any other day. As the evening came, he made it home. He was quiet and his eyes swollen with exhaustion. Not knowing what to say, I passed by him as he sat on the sofa and gently kissed his forehead. I sat beside him grabbing his hand when something happened. As I grabbed his hand and placed it on my cheek while closing my eyes, He said, "I'm tired honey. I need a break." I apologized for his exhaustion and obvious burn out while continuing to hold his hand as that was all I could think to do. To sit and be burned out with him.

While our officers may feel burnout, there are times we feel burnout too. Sometimes life is too much, and it seems as if there is no time in the day. There are also times where it is a never ending repetition of each day, the same schedule with no change. It is like a never ending cycle. We may look to people for comfort or find it in other ways, when in fact we need someone to stand with us, to sit with us in our exhaustion. God is the only one who meets us right where we are at and lets His heart break until ours is healed. In burnout receiving an extension of God's love through others can bring us relief and give us a sense of strength. There are also times when we are called to be the hands and feet of Jesus to those who are feeling exhausted. When faced with burnout, it is important to rest and allow God to pour into you. Silence can be golden when the world and daily demands are too loud for you and your precious heart. Allow God to give you rest and refresh your spirit each day. There will be times when the daily demands will have to wait and sitting at the feet of Jesus will be necessary in this life. Never be too busy that you forget about a very important person, you.

He gives strength to the weary and increases the power of the weak.

-Isaiah 40:29

Today's Prayer:

Lord,

When burnout hits me renew my strength. Give me the strength to carry on in your power. Increase the power of my officer each day on the beat. Allow us both to rest in the shelter of your arms. May I be an extension of your love to those who find themselves exhausted and weary. Father, please surround me with those who will be an extension of your love in my life. Thank you for graciously giving us strength and renewing us. Refresh my spirit and my mind. Renew my heart.

Amen

Today's Reflections:

_____

_____

_____

_____

_____

_____

_____

_____

_____

_____

_____

_____

_____

_____

_____

_____

_____

_____

_____

_____

_____

BEAUTIFUL WIFE ON DUTY, GOD MAKES ALL THINGS WORK TOGETHER FOR YOUR GOOD!

-ROMANS 8:28

DAY 18
DESIRES OF THE HEART
Dreaming hearts are beautiful beats to an amazing destiny.

One night my officer took me out for a little dinner date. As we sat there, we discussed grandkids although our children are literally babies, our dreams and hopes, and where we see ourselves when we are old and gray. My officer then said, "If I died soon, would you remarry?" I laughed and said, "Right away!" As he laughed at my response, I was shocked because it brought tears to my eyes. He asked me what was wrong, that it was just a question, when I replied, "Because I can't get this twice. Who can really get what we have twice in one life? I am sure I could find love again, but never would it be the love you and I have shared and have." He smiled his gentle smile and my heart melted. Our little dinner changed after that question, it became more intimate than it had started out. So each bite we took from our meal, each time we laughed, what we spoke of, to the precious moment we held hands to pray and bless our food, we absorbed each second.

As police wives we know full well our time with our officer and those we hold precious is not guaranteed. We should strive to never take those we love and the time we have for granted, but as humans, it happens. It can happen to all of us. Let's absorb all we can with what time we have. Life is too short and too precious to allow it to become fast paced. Your heart was made to dream and to have visions of what you hope for. A dreaming heart is a beautiful beat away from destiny. God places desires in your heart and wants to bless you with them as you delight in Him. When you trust God and do good, cultivating yourself in faithfulness, the Lord will grant you the desires of your heart. While you may have dreams and visions for your future, God's word says no mind could conceive, and no ear has ever heard the plans He has for those who love Him. While you dream big, God's plans are bigger. What you envision now, God's vision is even greater!

Take delight in the LORD, and He will give you the desires of your heart.

-Psalm 37:4

Today's Prayer:

Lord,

Help me to be content in all circumstances. As you guide me through this life, may the desires of my heart line up with your word. May my heart beat with yours and may my dreams and aspirations be yours. For my marriage and family, grant us your blessing as we have we hope for the future and all it holds. I take delight in you and love you for being our future holder. I release all dreams and visions to you and may your will be done in each of them.

Amen

Today's Reflections:

_____

_____

_____

_____

_____

_____

_____

_____

_____

_____

_____

_____

_____

_____

_____

_____

_____

_____

_____

_____

_____

_____

THIS WIFE ON DUTY LIFE IS NOT JUST FULL OF KEVLAR, GUNS, AND CUFFS. IT'S ABOUT THE AMAZING MAN BEHIND THESE THINGS AND THE LOVE I HAVE FOR HIM.

DAY 19
YOU HAVE THE RIGHT TO REMAIN SILENT
Arguing gets us nowhere, releasing gets us somewhere.

Arguing is a timeless marital act where two gather in a stand-off to discover who is right and who is wrong. It was a hot Texas summer day when my officer arrived home. The door slammed shut and exhaustion filled the air. We were two tired people who felt as if our day was busier than the other. So the argument began, who really had the longer and harder day? After all was said and done, tears rolled down my cheeks and I wondered why I had not just remained silent. It was obvious we were both exhausted, and the argument held no value, it was pointless. Then the thought came, "Arguing will get me nowhere, but releasing it to God will get me somewhere."

Sometimes we must remain silent. Words can be so great, yet, they can cause harm. Have you ever found yourself in an argument only to find that it was not worthy of concern? Arguing isn't designated strictly for marriage, but can also be done with those we are around each day, including social media pages. Remaining silent is like its own duty belt, not everyone can carry it. However, silence is like a Kevlar vest that we must wear as an invisible shield to protect our hearts. Arguing is seen as a defense mechanism, something we feel needs to be expressed and not silenced. But as our officer gears up physically for duty, we should gear up mentally and spiritually. When we gear up spiritually, we can focus on peace and understand what it means to release it to God. He will direct us to know when we need to speak and when we need to remain silent. When we speak, it should be filled with truth, love, and grace. Releasing any bitterness, frustrations, or an argument we are withholding will take us to a place of peace. When we release it, our eyes open to see the matter through the eyes of God and it takes the blindness out of our thought process.

Take control of what I say, O LORD, and guard my lips.

-Psalm 141:3

Today's Prayer:

Lord,

For arguments, give me peace and help me to not be one of reaction. Remind me that when I start a quarrel, I am opening a floodgate. Forgive me for those times I began an argument not worth having. May the Holy Spirit guide my family and I in knowing when we need to speak and when we need to remain silent. May my words be used for building up and not tearing down. As words flow from my mouth, let them be a blessing and not a curse. May all my words point back to you as you guard my lips.

Amen

Today's Reflections:

_____

_____

_____

_____

_____

_____

_____

_____

_____

_____

_____

_____

_____

_____

_____

_____

_____

_____

_____

_____

_____

_____

AS A WIFE ON DUTY BE ON GUARD; STAND FIRM IN THE FAITH; BE COURAGEOUS; BE STRONG

-1 Corinthians 16:13

DAY 20
UNFRIENDED

God didn't call us to be approved by all, but live in peace with all.

In a social media driven world and movements determined whose life matters most, we have found in law enforcement that approval by others is a challenge. As police wives we have struggled in scrolling through the news feeds and reading comments left by the very citizens, our officers serve and protect. We have experienced prejudice, leaving us with a sense of frustration and anger. If only we could make others understand, but that is a battle we will never win. This does not strictly apply to being a law enforcement family, but being who we are as an individual. You were placed in this world to stand out. There will be people in your life who disagree with you, those who are not your biggest fan, and those who just don't understand.

Lack of understanding and disagreements lead us to unfriend or be unfriended by those we hold dear or are acquainted with. We separate ourselves without realizing God never called us to be approved by all, but to be at peace with all. Disagreements, opinions, and points of view are all a part of free will. These opinions and passions are not expressed with respect, causing division. But what are we to do when we find ourselves at unrest and emotionally bitter towards another? When someone hurts or frustrates us we should forgive, however, it is not always easy. Forgiveness takes time, but worth it if you want to be at peace not just with others, but within yourself. God wants you to radiate His grace so that others will see it through your actions, words, or decisions. In all circumstances seek the best possible way to bring and discover an opportunity of peace. Even when you are rejected, God is boldly beside you. Be a peacekeeper and watch wonders unfold. When others are against you, you will tear down walls with a response of peace, not by your work, but by the work of a peaceful God.

Never pay back evil with more evil. Do things in such a way that everyone can see you are honorable. Do all that you can to live in peace with everyone.

-Romans 12:18

Today's Prayer:

Lord,

It is so hard to be at peace with those who have offended or hurt me in any way. Work in my heart so I may be a person of peace and grace. Thank you for giving me peace when I need it most. Thank you for your grace because I know I am not worthy of it, yet you give it so freely. In any disagreement, help me to show your love and refuse to repay evil with evil. Forgive me for the times I failed in this area. Let my life be one is at peace with others.

Amen

Today's Reflections:

_____

_____

_____

_____

_____

_____

_____

_____

_____

_____

_____

_____

_____

_____

_____

_____

_____

_____

_____

_____

_____

_____

_____

A Wife On Duty Vow

This Wife On Duty Takes Thee To Be Mine.
To Have And To Hold As We Walk The Thin Blue
Line.
In Sickness And Health, Till Death Do Us Part,
I Will Continuously Pursue Your Heart.
I Will Stand By You When You Honor The Fallen.
Be Understanding When Duty Gets To Callin'.
I Will Be Strength When You Are Weak.
Be Your Back Up In Prayer As You Guard The
Beat.
I Will Cover You With Love And Cuff Your Hand
In Mine,
All The While Never Letting Go As We Walk This
Thin Blue Line.

CUFFS SECURE, DETAIN, HOLD TOGETHER, AND NEVER ALLOW SEPARATION. I PRAY MY MARRIAGE WOULD BE CUFFED IN LOVE, GRACE, JOY, AND EVERY SECOND OF MY MARRIAGE WOULD BE FILLED WITH UNITY.

A FIRST RESPONDER MARRIAGE CUFFED IN GOODNESS.

DAY 21
BLESSED ARE THE PEACEKEEPERS
Peacekeeping is not just a call for my officer, but a call for me too.

Blessed are the peacemakers. We hear that phrase constantly, see it on photos that feature our first responders, but that word is not just for them. Could it be for us too as wives on duty? Yes! In every marriage there are times of irritability and crankiness. If you have not experienced this, you are a miracle! One morning my officer woke up slightly grumpy. I didn't get the usual, "Good morning my love" that I am use to on his days off. Instead I got a glance, half smirk, and a "Hey." I thought, "Oh boy, we got a mood here." I proceeded with my morning and all it entailed. All the while, my officer was silent, emotionless, motionless, and honestly I wasn't sure what to think. So I did what any normal wife would do and allowed all kinds of negativity to enter my mind. A battle began. I would say, "NO! God, give him a spirit of joy, peace, and sound mind." Then the thoughts would come back. It was an ongoing battle until I saw the words on a plaque in our home that read, "Blessed are the peacemakers! Could it be? Was God reminding me I was to be the peacemaker? I laughed and said, "Ok

God, I get it, but how?" My officer loves coffee, so I made him a cup. He looked at me with a blank face and said, "Thank you." I walked off and SWAT!!! A smack to the rear I got! I turned around and he winked his eye and said, "Good morning my love." Your spouse is not the only peacekeeper in your home. You too are called to be a peacekeeper. You can either cave in allowing your circumstances to rule, or you can speak God's word and let Him rule. It takes action to be a peacemaker along with creating a peaceful tone, outcome, or solution. We are quick to battle the wrong things or people. Perhaps you will be the only peace others see. It is important to challenge yourself in this area. In a chaotic world you must step back to see beyond the actions and words of others. Too often we get consumed in life staying focused more on ourselves and missing the underlying cries for help others are expressing. Stay alert and be ready, for you were called to be a peacekeeper.

Blessed are the peacemakers for they shall be called the children of God.

-Matthew 5:9

Today's Prayer:

Lord,

May I be a vessel you work through for living in peace. Use my mouth, hands, and feet to extend peace graciously to all I have access to. As my officer patrols the beat give him peace as he enters the chaotic. I know you do not give as the world gives and I praise you for that. Continuously give me your peace in all circumstances. Leave my family and I with a peace that surpasses all understanding. Thank you father for being the peace we need.

Amen

Today's Reflections:

_____

_____

_____

_____

_____

_____

_____

_____

_____

_____

_____

_____

_____

_____

_____

_____

_____

_____

_____

_____

_____

_____

_____

_____

_____

DO NOT LOSE HEART!
THOUGH OUTWARDLY YOU
ARE WASTING AWAY,
INWARDLY YOU ARE BEING
RENEWED
DAY BY DAY.
-2 Corinthians 4:16-18

DAY 22
SHARING SACRIFICE
Sharing Your Heart Isn't Just Words, But In What You Let Go Of.

The countdown began...10, 9, 8, 7, 6, 5, 4, 3, 2, 1, HAPPY NEW YEAR!! I grabbed a shirt from the basket and folded clothes. Auld Lang Syne played in the background. I remember being home alone and folding laundry as I watched everyone celebrating, laughing, and kissing on live television. A new year had arrived and while I felt this celebration in my heart, there was a sense of loneliness. I walked into our baby's room to kiss his warm cheeks when my phone rang. It was my officer! "Happy New Year Honey, I love you! Gotta go!" With excitement I said I loved him back before he hung up. Fireworks filled the sky as I could see them from the window, yet I stood alone in our little apartment. Even with my officer at a distance, he was still present in my heart. While it hurt me to not have him home, I remembered why I support his duty and allowed myself to let him go.

During special occasions and holidays, many police wives find themselves alone because duty calls. While there are no words to bring you out of that silent moment or even sense of loneliness, please know, countless wives on duty understand. Our holidays and special occasions are never set as the world sees, but set according to "our" time. In life we will have moments where our loneliness drowns us and almost feels like an affliction. But if we look beyond our personal emotion, we will see those moments connect us on a deeper level with a heart of sacrifice. As individuals we support others in their decisions, life call, and goals. When we give such support, it removes selfishness and we realize our support goes beyond what is best for us, even if it means standing alone. When those we love and support are not near, there is no distance too great where their heart is not connected with ours. Sharing your heart isn't just words spoken, but in what you let go of for the sake of the other. As a law enforcement wife, it takes a special person to share the one their heart loves with their very own city. You share your heart and allow your officer to walk out the door each day. While it is difficult, remember your sacrifice doesn't go unnoticed. When you also support others, know your support is assisting the other in reaching their destiny. Your support and encouragement is needed in someone's life, just as you need it in your own. Without such support, many would fail.

And do not forget to do good and to share with others, for with such sacrifices God is pleased.

-Hebrews 13:16

Today's Prayer:

Lord,

As I encourage my officer and others, remind me that support may also mean sacrifice. When I am left standing alone to find myself in sadness, replace it with joy and peace. Connect my heart to yours so it will connect with others on a level of love and respect. Remind me what it means to be a wife on duty when I forget. Guide me and strengthen me. Thank you for always remaining by my side in times of solitude.

Amen

Today's Reflections:

WHEN THE BEAT HAS BEEN PATROLLED, THE VELCRO RIPPED OFF, THE GUNBELT HUNG UP, THE RADIO BECOMES SILENT, AND BOOTS ARE OFF...IT IS IN THAT MOMENT WE BECOME "US". IT IS THE OFF DUTY "US" I LOOK FORWARD TO EACH DAY.

DAY 23
DIFFERENT LEVELS
In Due Time The Lord Is Found

It was Mother's Day, and the pastor asked all the husbands to stand up and bless their wives. Each pew was filled and one by one men rose to their feet to lay hands of prayer over their wives. I remember the heart sinking feeling as I tried to hold back tears. While I enjoyed church on Sundays, I dreaded attending alone. My officer was not a church going man and my heart longed for the day he would sit beside me. I longed for Him to know the Lord. I knew I could not change his heart. I prayed understanding that God was a journey he would have to discover and long for himself. I recalled the events leading me to Christ and God reminded me, "In due time, just like you, He will find me."

So many of us pray and long for our spouse, a child, friend, or loved one who will come to know the Lord the way we do. Far too often we try to force God on others when all we need to do is love them. By showing them love and compassion we allow God to move through our love. Perhaps our forcefulness would lead them astray and cause us to impede what God is trying to do. God is a revealer of many things. His love is first expressed and experienced when we find him. When we have an individual in our life who we want to see saved in the Lord, we must pray for them to be surrounded by those who know His truth and word. Many times it will not be us who lead them Christ, but our prayers and patient love. It is all about releasing them into mightier hands and trusting that their journey will begin when their heart is ready. When you radiate God's love and hold the joy only He can give, those around you will want what you have. They will not want the material things you get, but the joy you have that can only be found in Jesus Christ. It can be a long wait when we want to see others in the Lord, but it is worth the wait when we witness their discovery in Him. Sometimes we need to step aside so God can be by their side. God is not forceful, He is gentle. God is not in our face, but he longs to see our face. We must pray for those we hold precious to seek His face and in doing so we will witness God's unchanging love for them. It's not their actions and bad behaviors necessarily, but that the enemy is blinding them. Most times we pray about others actions when we should pray for their vision. With spiritual eyes open is when they see a savior is needed. When that occurs, salvation comes and from there, their actions or behaviors will line up with the word of God.

This is good, and pleases God our Savior, who wants all people to be saved and to come to a knowledge of the truth.

-1 Timothy 2:3-4

Lord,

As I pray for those lost in my life, I ask that you would remove all blindness and open their eyes to see your face. Help me to speak with gentleness and grace when I am with them. Love them through me and use me in such a way that draws them to you. I declare that my family will be saved and those who I am praying and believing salvation for.

Amen

Today's Reflections:

WHEN YOU CRY TO THE LORD IN YOUR TROUBLES, HE WILL SAVE YOU FROM DISTRESS.

-Psalm 107:19

DAY 24
BULLET PROOF VEST
May You Gear Up For The Days Of Battle

There may be some of you pleading, crying out, finding yourself in a time of desperation. You must know God has heard you, He hears you, and He is with you. From our own human sight we cannot see the impossible, but we can believe for it and pray for it. It is then, God himself does it. Sometimes it takes a final fight in you to make the change. It takes those pleas, tears, and groans to rise higher, to overcome, and be awakened. So, wake up. Open your eyes and dare to see what others cannot. Let the tears represent cleansing and healing. Time to start now, time to fight in prayer. The battle is not yours, it God's. In relentless trials, we need a bulletproof vest.

Just as the officer stands firm dressed in battle gear, so shall you stand firm against the tactics of the enemy. When he lurks like a lion, you will be wise and know when to shield yourself. Battles are not just physically present but spiritually too. When we think of gearing up, we often think of items or a form of clothing. When trials come, we also see that the target is not always physically present. In the presence of battle the gear God asks us to wear is called the armor of God. When we ask God to clothe us in it, we ask him to give us certain protection in six distinct forms. These forms are the shield of truth, the helmet of salvation, the breastplate of righteousness, the belt of truth, the shoes of peace, and the sword of the spirit. Even when your heart fails the heartbeat of God will keep you alive. Many bullets of defeat will shoot your way, but the Lord has prepared your very own battle gear sweet wife on duty. As you dress each day, remember the most important pieces you put on will be not cloth, but armor.

Therefore put on the full armor of God, so that when the day of evil comes, you may stand your ground, and after you have done everything, to stand. Stand firm then, with the belt of truth buckled around your waist, with the breastplate of righteousness in place, and with your feet fitted with the readiness that comes from the gospel of peace. Besides all this, take up the shield of faith, with which you can extinguish all the flaming arrows of the evil one.

Take the helmet of salvation and the sword of the Spirit, which is the word of God. And pray in the Spirit on all occasions with all kinds of prayers and requests. With this in mind, be alert and always keep on praying for all the Lord's people.

-Ephesians 6: 10-18

Today's Prayer:

Lord,

As I face trials in this life, remind me you have given us your full armor. As I gear up for the battles of life, give me strength to fight on my knees in prayer. I trust you with my life and all the battles that come my way. I thank you for the victory I hold in you. As my officer gears up, I pray he never depends on his bulletproof vest, but on you, the ultimate protector. May we always turn to you for protection, especially in the days of darkness. Remind me it was never my battle to fight, but yours.

Amen

Today's Reflections:

_____

_____

_____

_____

_____

_____

_____

_____

_____

_____

_____

_____

_____

_____

_____

_____

_____

_____

_____

_____

_____

_____

_____

AS A WIFE ON DUTY,
MY HAND WILL ALWAYS
REACH FOR HIS.
AFTER EVERY SHIFT,
HEARTACHE, OR STRUGGLE.

DAY 25
PARTNER IN CRIME
The One Friend I Can Depend On Through All Seasons, Is Jesus Christ

There will be people in our lives we cross paths with who will remain with us for a short or long time. We have had friends who text constantly, invite you for a girls night out, or even listen as you unload all your annoyances and excitements. While we would love for people to remain in our lives consistently, it isn't so. Once upon a precious time, a friend of mine would show up at my door with coffee in one hand and her children in the other. It was always such a blessing to see her. She was the smile my day needed. She was the one person who knew me in all my realness, my partner in crime. No matter what I shared, she listened and never judged. Her phone was always on and no matter the time. But one day, I realized something, we had not spoken in a long while. The daily demands had taken us both and what we once knew as friendship became nonexistent. It brought sadness to my heart, and with multiple attempts to reconnect, it never happened. New friends came along and occupied our time, leaving me with a resolve that all people have a season in my life.

There will be a time when your partner in crime is no longer around. Perhaps time drifted you apart or maybe even a disagreement occurred. When these things happen, it can almost feel like rejection or even leave you with questions like, "What happened?" God brings people into your life for different seasons and reasons. There are no chance meetings. When someone crosses your path, they are there to either encourage you, grow you, lead, or even walk with you through specific times in your life. Each of us have a destiny to fulfill and not everyone can go where you go. It will take certain people that God will use to be his hands and feet in your life. When their season is up, it's ok, not everyone can remain. There will be a constant flow of friendships and with each one thank God for all lessons learned and love received. Each friendship will be unique and serve a purpose that will be perfect for the season you are in. There must be a balance in friendships and while it is nice to have numerous friends, it is important to keep your circle small. God will remove people from your life and it is important not to chase them down. Not everyone will be a benefit. Always ask God to bring the right people into your life. If there are disagreements causing a friendship to end, it is important to make peace with that person before parting ways. Friendship is a blessing and can be so valuable. But, the one friend we can depend on that remains with us through all seasons, is Jesus Christ.

As iron sharpens iron, so one person sharpens another.

-Proverbs 27:17

Today's Prayer:

Lord,

Thank you for the friendships I have had in life. As I enjoy those friendships, may I also be a friend who blesses and encourages others in their season of need. Surround me with those who will sharpen me to become all you need me to be. May I also sharpen those around me.

Amen

Today's Reflections:

Who can find a virtuous wife on duty? For she is far more precious than jewels. As she learns to embrace more often, fighting the fear of no return. For her officer goes above and beyond for his city, yet she goes above and beyond for him. It is a journey they both venture on, with the unknown ahead. But yet, there is a certainty that her officer will never be alone. For she is a wife on duty and so much more. She is the one who is always one step behind. She is the one who will journey this life, with boldness and strength. Thank you for all you do wives on duty! Thank you for the countless unseen things you do daily. Thank you for the sacrifices you make. Thank you even when it becomes too much to bear. You are far more precious than jewels.

God will direct your steps by His word and let no iniquity have dominion over you.

-Psalm 119:133

DAY 26
MISSED TARGET
The Enemy Will Try To Bring You Down When You're At Your Best.

Our officers are trained to focus on the task at hand. Each call will be filled with much detail and distractions all around. However, the eye of an officer is sharp, diligent, and on target. Any distraction allowed could mean harm or a missed piece of evidence. It could keep them from their goal of bringing peace or solving the crime! Full focus on what is before an officer is crucial for not only survival, but also for knowledge. Distractions in life are always present. They come in many forms. They can be as thoughts, emotions, illness, or many unnecessary tasks. However, we must remember to focus on what is true, honorable, knowledgeable, and the goal. The enemy will try to bring us down when we are at our best because he knows we can miss our target when we are not focused.

There will always be new creations, new distractions. It is what you do with those things that matters most. You can either use it to your advantage or make it a disadvantage in your life. Too often we set resolutions or high expectations for ourselves, leading us to failure because of distraction. But no matter what, there is nothing that can separate you from the grace of God! Sometimes we want to start off running toward our goals when in fact we must walk to get there. It is important to pace yourself. Expect to do the great and mighty things you have been called to, but know it will take steps. While distractions may come, don't be hard on yourself, instead love yourself. Target practice will be necessary to achieve and help you stay focused. You will need to practice saying, "no" or learn healthy habits. Don't miss your evidence, God is always speaking to you. Keep an eye out for treasures only God can give throughout your day. When we take our focus off the goal, we derail. Seek God by asking Him to establish your steps and to help you remain focused on Him. The lord says His sheep know His voice. It is important to listen, and even more important to focus. When we remain focused, we can serve God best! God's grace will keep you on track when you get off course, so keep seeking His will.

I am saying this for your benefit, not to place restrictions on you. I want you to do whatever will help you serve the Lord best, with as few distractions as possible.

-1 Corinthians 7:35

Today's Prayer:

Lord,

With all the distractions in life, help me stay focused. Help me to remain on target in all things you have called me to. Give me vision to see distractions for what they are and remove them. Fine tune my ears to hear your voice. Lead me in making healthy habits that allow me to focus on what is important. When I get off course, set my feet back to the right path. I know you are bigger than the enemy and I thank you for giving me authority over him. May you be my focus in all things and my truth in all circumstances.

Amen.

Today's Reflections:

_____

_____

_____

_____

_____

_____

_____

_____

_____

_____

_____

_____

_____

_____

_____

_____

_____

_____

_____

_____

*EVERY TEAR, EVERY PRAYER,
AND EVERY CRY IS HEARD.
GOD HOLDS A SPECIAL
PLACE FOR THOSE WHO
LOVE AN OFFICER.*

DAY 27
WHAT IF?
The "What If's" Of Life Cause Us To Live Uniquely

The scene couldn't have been more perfect. It was dark, the stars shined brightly, a bonfire was lit, and we had the ocean as our view. This vacation had differed from the others. My officer had done things for me I had always wished for. Those things I had casually mentioned I would love and even things mentioned as far back as when we were dating. I asked, "What made you do all of it at once?" He then said, "Because something could happen and I want to make sure I made you smile, happy, and gave you times you will always remember." I cried and there was a silence between us. The silence that spoke volumes about the love we share and yet the sadness and reality of the "what if" we live each day.

As wives on duty we can be thankful for even what is unseen. Their service goes far beyond the call of duty, but carries on in their homes and families. There is no doubt many of our officers often wonder, "What if something happens." Even with such a question they still pursue the darkest places to protect a world that so many are ungrateful for. Our officers see the world as it could be and not as it is. We can equally ask ourselves the same question. What if something happened to you? Has your life been lived in such a way that is pleasing to the Lord? Have your family and friends received the best of you? It is important to give love, but the love you give when no one is watching. Each day it is prayed that we make it home safe. This is not strictly for our officer, but for us, and those we love. We must laugh often, smile more, and pray we get the chance to do all things dreamt of. Precious words like, "I love you" need be said often and not withheld. We all have a destination and that is physical death. It is where the end meets legacy. It will not be what you left behind but what you left within the hearts of others. Memories are best made in the present.

So teach us to number our days that we may get a heart of wisdom.

-Psalm 90:12

Today's Prayer:

Lord,

Teach me to number my days so I may have a heart of wisdom. Give me opportunities to express love to those in my life. Don't allow the "what if's" to be something I fear, but to be something that causes me to action. While I may die physically, I have comfort in knowing I live eternally with you because you are my Lord and Savior. May I leave a legacy that goes beyond material things. As always protect me and those I love. May we all make it home safely each day to enjoy each other in laughter, smiles, and love.

Amen

Today's Reflections:

_____

_____

_____

_____

_____

_____

_____

_____

_____

_____

_____

_____

_____

_____

_____

_____

_____

_____

_____

_____

_____

_____

_____

_____

WHEN YOU WALK THROUGH THE FIRE, YOU WILL NOT BE BURNED; THE FLAMES WILL NOT SET YOU ABLAZE.

-Joshua 1:9

DAY 28

PRESSING CHARGES

It's in the pressing of time that God pulls us through.

As I ironed my officer's uniform I imagined all the mental and spiritual wrinkles I couldn't iron out. Wrinkles so deep and seen despite the heat and pressing I do in the physical. But what about those hidden wrinkles? Those stubborn wrinkles I see, yet can't get out? In our own lives we all have those wrinkles. It is almost like the enemy pressing charges against us. He charges us with fear or insecurity, hopelessness or condemnation, anger or frustration, and sometimes despair. Just as the physical wrinkles in his uniform can be straightened out with lots of heat and pressing, so can the things we face in our own lives. We get into heated situations, conversations, friendships or relationships, and even heated moments that causes us to burn to the core. But yet, heat rises and in each of the trials we face, so can we. We can rise! As for the pressing, it's all about pressing forward and pushing to birth and make something new. It's all about perspective in the daily wrinkles of life. We can try ironing things out ourselves, or we can let God do it for us.

It's in the heat and fire that God himself stood with the three (Daniel 3:25). It is in the pressing of time that God pulls us through. Let us pray for the mental

143

and spiritual wrinkles we cannot reach. Many of us have been accused or labeled. While those who accuse us may leave a bitterness, we are not called to dewrinkle or fix anyone. We are called to pray. Once we have prayed we can then assist, love, and care for those around us, including our enemies. The dewrinkling God who smooths everything out and makes it beautiful, is the one whom you should trust. Today and every day, leave all your wrinkles in mighty hands. Time to let God. Let him iron it out. Let God walk with you through the fires of life. It is in the heart and fire where you become more refined. It is in the testing of time where you pass.

See, I have refined you, though not as silver; I have tested you in the furnace of affliction.

-Isaiah 48:10

Today's Prayer:

Lord,

Even when the enemy accuses me of much, it is you who refines me. Even though I walk through the fires of affliction, I know you will never leave me. Help me to shine in the darkest of places and see that the wrinkles of life can be used for my benefit. Refine me and my family to our greatest brilliance. Remind me to leave those who accuse or label me in your mighty hands. As I live freely in your grace, may I extend grace to others as I know they too have struggles. I trust I will rise with you when times are pressing.

Amen

Today's Reflections:

_____

_____

_____

_____

_____

_____

_____

_____

_____

_____

_____

_____

_____

_____

_____

_____

_____

_____

_____

_____

_____

I WILL BE MY OFFICER'S CHAMPION IN THE GOOD TIMES AND BAD.

DAY 29
RETURN TO DUTY
Even After Time Has Passed, God Gets Us To The Next Step

It's the first day. First day of what you ask? The first day my officer hits the beat again after tragedy. I don't know, something is different. There is a racing in my heart, there is a battle in my mind between peace and anxiety. There is the absorption in my ears listening to the comforting noises of Velcro, zips, buckles, and then just like that...he's ready. But I am not sure I am ready to let him go. We looked at each other and no words were necessary because my eyes screamed, "Come home safe! Please!" And his embrace told me, "I will. I can't promise, but I will." So, he left, and I stayed. As he drove away I sighed as my heart beat a little harder and under my breath I whispered, "God, please." And in some amazing way I heard God's voice, "I'm here. Let's do this day together."

As a wife on duty we must send those desperate whispers to a God who is bigger. Those whispers change our focus. There will be many first days after recovering from an injury or after a tragedy. Those days make letting go so much harder. But each time will mean a different emotion leaving us to release them to a never changing God. When we experience such days, we should remind ourselves that God gives strength to the weary and increases the power of the weak. Though you grow weary, tired, and fall in exhaustion, because you trust in the Lord, He will renew your strength. After facing a major change, injury, or tragedy, moving forward can be a challenge. But even after time has passed, God gets us to the next step. He never asks us to rush, but to be in step with Him as He leads. In life we will have "return to duty" moments. It is always uncomfortable, it may feel unstable, and can cause uncertainty. When we feel in such a way, God is always there to walk it with you, leading you one step at a time.

Your word is a lamp for my feet, a light on my path.

-Psalm 119:105

Today's Prayer:

Lord,

Your word is precious and is the light I need as I take each step in life. In all the return to duty moments, give me courage to move forward. Give me the confidence and boldness to walk in your name. Let not fear rule my life, but peace. I invite you to walk with me each day. I ask that you forgive me if I have failed to ask you to be a part of the wondrous day you made. Renew my strength and increase power in me when I fall weak. Thank you for being the same yesterday, today, and forever more.

Amen

Today's Reflections:

_____

_____

_____

_____

_____

_____

_____

_____

_____

_____

_____

_____

_____

_____

_____

_____

_____

_____

_____

_____

_____

_____

_____

ALLISON P. URIBE

ANGELS ARE WATCHING OVER YOU AND YOUR OFFICER

-Psalm 91:11-12

DAY 30
THE THIN BLUE LINE
Even When Others Are Against You, God Is For You

Our officers stand with the riot shield fighting the crowds of protesters. As they fight against the wave of people yelling and expressing such anger, they stand guard facing them head on and not once do we see them break. They have a duty to perform and they will fulfill it. One will never see them put the shield down or stand hurt in a corner because they are being yelled or cursed at. The visual of our officers in those circumstances teach us something about how to stand against adversity.

As we face such things as hatred, we too must take up our own shield and fight it for what it is. We know the words others may speak or think about our law enforcement are not of truth. Not all officers are perfect and some will fail, but this does not define the majority. Therefore, although those words may stir up anger, we can have a sense of pride knowing how noble they really are. Our son came home one day asking if all police officers were bad. We were puzzled at the question and came to find he was told this in school. A little girl told him her dad said all officers were bad. He was hurt by those words and said, "My daddy isn't bad." We comforted him and explained how others have opinions, yet they held no weight. We encouraged him to believe what he knew to be true about his daddy, and those he serves with. We need not to convince another how incredible the duty of our warriors are because it is expressed each day they respond to the call. It is also shown when those speaking harsh words are protected by the one they curse. Since we know who our officers really are, we can save our breath for more worthwhile things, such as life. There will always be someone who has a negative comment to make or a judgement to pass. We can take it in or combat those lies with our shield of truth. By holding up our shield of truth, we can get a joy and celebrate the awesomeness of what God has called us to and who He has called us to be. It is always important to remember that God is for you and for your call in this life.

What shall we say in response to these things? If God is for us, who can be against us?

-Romans 8:31

Today's Prayer:

Lord,

Help me to take up the shield of truth in adversity. It is difficult being in a law enforcement family as we face the hatred of others. Give us shoes of peace as we walk this world. Give us amazing understanding and grace as we face it. Give us the strength to not fight evil with evil, but to know we are not fighting them, we are fighting the enemy. Fill us with truth so we can stand strong in love.

Amen

A Wife On Duty Promise

When they don't support you, I will.
When they hate you, I will love you.
When they don't appreciate you, I will be
grateful for you.
When they seek to harm you, I will cover
you in prayer.
When you are judged, you can depend on
my love.
When you break, I will hold you.
When you leave to the patrol the streets,
My heart will go with you.
When our city doesn't see the sacrifice you
make, it's ok, because I get to witness it
every day.

Today's Reflections:

_____

_____

_____

_____

_____

_____

_____

_____

_____

_____

_____

_____

_____

_____

_____

_____

_____

_____

_____

_____

_____

_____

_____

_____

THE BADGE I PROUDLY STAND BESIDE LIES ON HIS CHEST CLOSE TO HIS HEART, BECAUSE THIS CALL ON HIS LIFE AS AN OFFICER, TAKES HEART!

DAY 31
DETAINED

Detaining hurt will only keep one from moving forward.

I pulled off the band aid. There it was, a scar that wasn't gone and would probably remain. I thought about how many times we get hurt in life or even in marriage. We cover it up to avoid further pain or exposure to more harm. Many times we cover up our hearts or walk around masking all we have faced while never properly choosing healthy healing methods. Even though we cover up our hurt or pain, eventually that cover will come off and the wound will be exposed. That leaves us with a question; will it be painless or hurt all over again?

When hurting in life or in marriage, don't put a Band-Aid over a serious wound. Some wounds require healing and time. Ensure that what you cover your situation with, will not hurt more when exposed later. To detain pain is far from wise. Treat your hurt with care. Give it time. We have heard time heals all wounds. Does it really? We may find healing and be at a newer level, but we will always have that scar. The hurt we may experience can alter our behavior when we revisit that hurt, no matter how much time has passed. Healing will take as long as it takes. Since we have all experienced some hurt in our life or in marriage, whether it be through disconnection, disagreements, infidelity, or words, we can heal in a healthy way. We can do this by move forward. Detaining hurt will only keep us from progression. We need to seek someone to walk through the hurt with us. No one else could ever validate your pain, but it could be their listening ear or warm smile that gets you from one day to the next. As you carry on in your everyday life, there will be trials and scars both physically or emotionally. You need to seek not temporal fixes but permanent resolutions.

But he was pierced for our transgressions, he was crushed for our iniquities; the punishment that brought us peace was on him, and by his wounds we are healed.

-Isaiah 53:5

Today's Prayer:

Lord,

Remove all Band-Aids from the wounds of my heart. Guide me as I seek permanent resolutions, ridding myself of any temporal fixes. Place someone in my life who will walk with me and be a listening ear while giving godly wisdom. I no longer want to detain the hurts I have experienced, but instead I want to uncover them. I ask that you cover all pain with your grace. While I may be scarred, I know your love and what you did on the cross will bring healing. Thank you Jesus!

Amen

Today's Reflections:

GOD IS YOUR COMFORTER
BEAUTIFUL WIFE ON DUTY

-2 Corinthians 1:3-4

DAY 32
LICENSE AND REGISTRATION PLEASE
Would The Real You Please Stand Up?

As I strolled the beach with my son, we noticed a lot of beautiful shells. We grabbed our favorites and placed them in our bucket. He later came running with a shell split in half. He said, "Mommy, look at this! It's so beautiful but it's split in half. I guess we could try to glue it or just leave it here." As I looked at the shell, its beauty was unlike any other I had seen. Although it was split in half, each piece had its own unique beauty. I told my son, "It doesn't have to be put together or whole to be beautiful." In life, we will not always have it together, yet we will be beautiful because of who we belong to, and that's the creator of heaven and earth.

There will be moments you feel split in half or broken on some days. You must realize that it's ok! You may not always understand life. Like my son, you may think glue or putting yourself back together is the answer. That's not your job, that's God's. With God being the creator of all things, you are no accident and where you are in life now is no accident. It is brought upon by our free will and living in a fallen world. With all this, God has promised us beauty for ashes. Your family may not always have it together and you may face the storms of life, but you are promised beauty. Even in your brokenness, you are fearfully and wonderfully made, a masterpiece in the making. There will never be a need to put a mask on or perform for the world when God is by your side. Many people proclaim to have it all together and speak of not understanding those tears, but they are wrong. Each person, first responder and household has its own shares of struggle. There is no such thing as perfection. Acknowledge the many tears that are cried day in and day out. It is time to stop looking in the mirror, to stop listening to others opinions of you, to stop criticizing yourself, and to arise! Do not put your value in what the mirror reflects or how broken you feel. Put your value in God's print over your life. Put your value in the truth of who He says you are. You sweet wife on duty were born for great and mighty things. You are beautiful and the most wondrous masterpiece this world has ever seen, not because of your doing or the works you do, but because of God's work and His image. The image you are made of. Would the real you please stand up?

He has made everything beautiful in its time. He has also set eternity in the human heart; yet no one can fathom what God has done from beginning to end.

-Ecclesiastes 3:11

Today's Prayer:

Lord,

Even in my broken days, I know you have set eternity in my heart. Take the pieces of my life and make it beautiful. Thank you for loving me in all brokenness and help me to see myself through your eyes. Take any mask off that I wear and allow me to walk in the freedom of your grace. Be an umbrella over me. Help me to see my worth and who I am in you. Let my transparency bless others and yet allow me to receive blessings of encouragement.

Amen

Today's Reflections:

PRECIOUS WIFE.....
WIPE YOUR TEARS, TAKE A
DEEP BREATH, AND LIFT
YOUR HEAD UP TO THE
HILLS WHERE YOUR HELP
COMES FROM.

DAY 33

PEANUT BUTTER AND JELLY PATROL

When We Do Things For The Lord With Our Whole Heart,
It Blesses Many

A few years back, each night as my officer got into bed, he would yell out, "Don't forget my sandwich!" There were times I let out a sigh as I was too tired, but each time I would yell back, "I won't!" As I prepared it each night, I would smile as I knew exactly what that sandwich meant. While my officer would enjoy the sandwich on duty, it was also a blessing in so many unique ways. My attitude toward making them were not always good, especially if I was tired and just wanted to go to bed. It was until one day I forgot to make it. The next day I got a call from my officer and he was asking about it. I apologized to him and ensured he would have it the very next day. When I asked him why he wanted it so badly, his response changed my view completely. He mentioned that while on duty, there was a spot with a scenery so beautiful. When duty was slow, or he had no calls, he would go to this area to watch the sun rise and eat his sandwich. My heart hurt I had forgotten it that day. He said he got there, looked into his bag, and there was no sandwich. I then came to find out that these sandwiches also became a quick meal when it was too busy for him to eat. But the peanut butter and jelly adventures didn't stop there, these sandwiches had fed people he saw on the street who had no food.

We have a reminder in the word of God that whatever we do, we must do it wholeheartedly. Whatever we do, even the smallest things, we do it so our God is glorified. Even a peanut butter and jelly sandwich can make a huge difference when put to use as a blessing. There will be tasks and demands everywhere. We will find them in the workplace or even in the mundane things. Far too often we will never see the fruit of our labor. If we do it well and in love as for the Lord, there are no boundaries to where the blessings can go and how far it can reach.

Work willingly at whatever you do as though you were working for the Lord rather than for people.

-Colossians 3:23

Today's Prayer:

Lord,

Use my hands to do your work. Never allow me to be lazy or grumble at the thought of serving others. Take my heart and make it a place of blessing that extends to the world. Let the works of my hands be with open borders. May all things I do be done for you and for those you love. Forgive me if I have been disobedient to your call in any way for helping others. Transform my way of thinking as I fail to see just how big you are and that all things are for your glory.

Amen

Today's Reflections:

_____

_____

_____

_____

_____

_____

_____

_____

_____

_____

_____

_____

_____

_____

_____

_____

_____

_____

_____

_____

MAY GOD BE YOUR PLACE OF QUIET RETREAT AND YOU ALLOW HIS WORD TO RENEW YOU

-Psalm 119:14

DAY 34
POLICE LINE DO NOT CROSS
Boundaries are healthy for my family and life.

Schoolwork was being worked on and dinner was on the stove. My phone rang. I heard the notifications sound off and stopped what I was doing to see what was sent. As I read the text messages and noticed the missed calls, I could see there was a need. At the moment, I was consumed with my family, it was nearly impossible for me to leave. During that time, I said "yes" to everything and everyone. No one introduced me to a word called boundaries. The word "no" was given a reputation of being unacceptable. With the responsibilities I had, there was no other answer to give the person on the other end of the phone, but no. If only I could express how sorry I was and horrible I felt. I was neglecting someone in need. God gently reminded me that this person was never for me to care for, but for Him to care for. He was the only one who could reach her at the moment. He promised she wouldn't be helpless, but be put in a position where she could trust Him in all fullness.

Have you ever felt overwhelmed with the loads of others? While we are to carry each other's burdens, we are not called to carry their loads. Boundaries are healthy for your family and in life. Our family is our first ministry and we must protect that. We have our own load which will require our time and attention. We should test our actions and discover how boundaries are set according to our family needs. Many can do good works, but fail to do God's work. There are times we impede God revealing himself through miracles or even stretching someone's faith. Always seek to be obedient for helping others. It is important to direct those in need straight back to God. Far too often people become dependent on others, neglecting to see God as their provider. Boundaries set up a perimeter that will protect you and your family from overload. While we desire to say yes to so many, a simple no will allow you to pour into lives God has called you specifically to. No matter what, God cares for His children and your no will not mean they won't receive help, God is big enough to provide at any capacity.

Carry each other's burdens, and in this way you will fulfill the law of Christ. If anyone thinks they are something when they are not, they deceive themselves. Each one should test their own actions. Then they can take pride in themselves alone, without comparing themselves to someone else, for each one should carry their own load. The one who receives instruction in the word should share all good things with their instructor. Do not be deceived: God cannot be mocked. A man reaps what he sows.

-Galatians 6:2-7

Today's Prayer:

Lord,

As others call on me in need of help, give me wisdom on who you need me to assist. Help me to say no for caring for my family time and the responsibilities within my family. Give me strength to carry others burdens and encourage them to give their load to you. Guide me to what you need of me and know I will always be ready to help when you ask of me. Give me a vision of healthy boundaries in all areas of my life.

Amen

Today's Reflections:

_____

_____

_____

_____

_____

_____

_____

_____

_____

_____

_____

_____

_____

_____

_____

_____

_____

_____

_____

_____

_____

_____

A WIFE ON DUTY IS AN UNSEEN HERO WHO DISPLAYS SACRIFICE AND STRENGTH. SHE STRIVES TO BE A SUPPORT SYSTEM, HER OFFICER'S BIGGEST FAN, AN ENCOURAGER, AND WOUND HEALER.

DAY 35
BEYOND THE WORDS
Listening With Your Ears Will Also Require Listening With Your Heart

Listening requires focus and while we learn about what is being expressed, we gain knowledge of what's in the heart. I was cleaning around the house when I noticed my officer's odd silence. He usually arrived home with a smile, but this day was different. His smile was not so genuine and his demeanor was serious. I could always tell a good day from a bad one by the sounds made from the Kevlar vest. On a good day, the Velcro sounded quick and fast as if something was ripping apart. On a bad day, the Velcro sounded drawn out, as if he was trying to take it off without making a sound. That afternoon, the Velcro sounded like a bad day. I didn't want to force him to talk as I knew if he wanted to, he would eventually. He was never one to discuss his day on the beat, so I silently prayed. Dinner time came, and we ate with a few words spoken. As I put dishes in the sink, he looked at me and said, "Thank you". "For what?", I asked, and he responded, "I know you know I had a bad day, but I wasn't ready to talk about it and not sure I even want to talk about it. I am now." With a dish in hand

and a towel over my shoulder, I knew I had to stop what I was doing and focus on my officer. His eyes watered and his fists clenched as he spoke. I could only wonder what kind of mental battle he was facing. I could tell he was hurt and angry about the situation. After he shared what was on his heart, I heard him take a deep breath and noticed a sense of relief in his face. I held his hand, smiled, and gave him a hug.

Opportunities to listen will surround us each day. Although every person is different, it is vital to be ready and willing to listen when others are ready to speak. Listening will also help you to better understand what someone may have felt at the moment in case there is need for concern. When we listen, we can find many underlying meanings in what they say. Listening requires full attention, it is not just hearing. We may not always have the answers or solutions, but, listening is the answer and solution. Our ears are our greatest communication tool and our greatest ministry. Words expressed are never given without a heartfelt expression. Listening with your ears will also require listening with your heart.

Making your ear attentive to wisdom and inclining your heart to understanding.

-Proverbs 2:2

Today's Prayer:

Lord,

Make my ears attentive to wisdom and incline my heart to understanding. As others speak to me, give me insight to see any underlying meanings behind their words. Thank you for giving me ears as a part of life ministry. Help me to be quick to listen, slow to speak, and slow to anger. Fine tune my ears to not just listen to others, but to listen to the Holy Spirit.

Amen

*In the midst of trouble, in the midst of pain,
God will call a wife on duty by name. Her
tears may fall on the left and right, but God
himself will never give up the fight. For
when we feel weak, in his strength we rise. A
wife on duty will be given the ultimate prize.
For her sacrifice in this world is far greater
than any mind can conceive. To let go and
let God is what she chooses you see. Her
strength is great, her faith all the more, and
God himself will love her forever more.*

Today's Reflections:

_____

_____

_____

_____

_____

_____

_____

_____

_____

_____

_____

_____

_____

_____

_____

_____

_____

_____

_____

_____

_____

_____

Peace, I leave with you, my peace I give you. I do not give to you as the world gives. Do not let your hearts be troubled and do not be afraid.

-John 14:27

Day 36
GOOD NIGHT SWEETHEART
For Even In Our Greatest Hour Of Need, God Shows Up

Many years ago I remember walking into my bedroom to find my husband curled up in bed. He was quiet that day and his words were few to none. Back then I was still learning how to care for and love my husband who was now an officer. My views of his work differed greatly from what it is today, and I can only imagine how it will be years from now. On this day with a baby in my arms, I stared at the bed and sensed he was not asleep. Despite that, I said, "Goodnight sweetheart." I heard sniffling, felt a coldness in the air, and exited the room quietly. The sun was shining as it was four in the afternoon, and I kept wondering what happened. What could have brought my officer to such a moment of unwanted solitude? He never spoke of what happened that day and I never asked, but I knew he must have experienced something horrific. I was sure his mind couldn't comprehend what he had seen and could only imagine the images replaying over and over again.

From time to time that familiar silence may visit our homes. It is then we should pray. We should pray that despite it all, God will give our officer a vision like no other. When horrific experiences and tragedy lead us to solidarity, there is almost nothing that can bring us out of that darkness. Many times we experience depression leaving us in silence and separating ourselves from those we love. In such circumstances help is vital. As we cry to the Lord in our deepest pain, sometimes our tears speak louder than our words. It is always wise to pray for those we see in such a pit of sadness, including ourselves. It is equally important to seek help from others. In those times it is important to not get caught up in loneliness, but strive to reach out so others can walk with us. As the scripture says we will lie down in peace and sleep, we remember that it is in the shelter of God's safety where we will find such peace. It should be a prayer we all ask not just for ourselves, but for those we know are suffering. For even in the hour of our greatest need, God shows up. Perhaps you are the answer to someone's prayer by showing up and being with them. You can be someone's miracle and be the one who walks them to the light of day.

In peace I will lie down and sleep, for you alone, LORD, make me dwell in safety.

-Psalm 4:8

Today's Prayer:

Lord,

Thank you for the safety where I know I can dwell. As my officer and I lay down to sleep, may we sleep in your peace. If depression were to come, give us a hope that brings us to light. In our sadness, hold us so close to your heart. In our hour of need is where I know we can trust you. Use me to reach the hurting and send others when I am hurting. You are faithful and good at all times in our life. Continue to overtake us.

Amen

Today's Reflections:

_____

_____

_____

_____

_____

_____

_____

_____

_____

_____

_____

_____

_____

_____

_____

_____

_____

_____

_____

_____

HOPE IS WHAT I CLING TO IN THIS WIFE ON DUTY LIFE!

DAY 37
THE DAILY BULLETIN
God Doesn't Need Our Words Or Help To Bring A Trial To A Resolution

I recall a time when our marriage was in a dark place. I was frustrated with my officer and irritated beyond belief. A friend of mine stopped by our house to drop off cookies. She asked if I was ok as she noticed my irritability. I remember looking right at her and saying, "I am, but would be so much better if my husband wasn't such a jerk." She had this blank look on her face I will never forget. I walked off with this bitter taste in my mouth, and feeling horrible as I realized the words I spoke were something I couldn't take back. I went inside and as I walked in, tears rolled down my cheeks. I looked at my husband as he stared blankly at the television set. I had never felt so lost. The night went on and another opportunity came to respond differently. My mother had called to check on me. She also asked how my officer was doing and I responded with a simple "ok". I fought back the temptation to vent out all my frustrations and by the time I hung up, I felt numb. The next time I saw my friend it was awkward. I apologized for the words I spoke that night and while she said it was fine, I told her it definitely was not.

We can get so burnt out that venting seems like a quick and easy solution. God's word mentions that a fool will vent, but a wise man will remain quiet. It is not for judgment, but for protection. Once we release words of anger or frustration about another, we cannot get them back. We then allow people who do not know our story, our spouse or marriage, and people who are not wise, to pour their advice or opinion into the most sacred parts of our life. We remember that God knows your heart and the hearts of others. God goes to battle in our stillness. He is the one who brings change. He doesn't need our words or help to bring the trial to a resolution. He is God and we are not. Wives on duty, this is a struggle and while we may think we have a place we can "go to", please remember God is bigger. Find a superb, godly friend who will believe for miracles with you and encourage you. You want someone who will rejoice with you and love you and your spouse in the midst of your failures. So today please consider your words when speaking or posting about anything involving your life. In your wisdom you will find the world cannot access your marriage or life.

"A fool vents all his anger, a wise man keeps it back quietly."

- Proverbs 29:11

Today's Prayer:

Lord,

Help me to remain silent when I find myself angry. Remind me I can vent to you and you will move in my circumstances. Forgive me for all harsh words I have ever spoken toward anyone or about anyone. I pray I will not be moved by ungodly advice or opinions, but instead focus on your word and its wisdom. Surround me with those who will believe for miracles with me and give me godly counsel. Thank you for giving me peace when I ask.

Amen

Today's Reflections:

SOMETIMES YOU HAVE TO GRAB HIS KEVLAR, SQUEEZE IT TIGHT, AND PRAY HARD.

DAY 38
MASCARA ON MY PILLOW
Teardrops On My Pillow Is A Sign That Healing Took Place

Have you ever woke up to find mascara on your pillow from tears? The night before tears ran down your face as you hugged your pillow tight. So many tissues crumbled and you find that each tear represents something so different in your life. There will be times when this life is something we want to give up, times when we find we are ever so proud of it, times when fear takes over, and there will be times when we have no emotion or thought over it. It is what it is.

My eyes were swollen as I struggled to open them from the sadness of the night before. Our family had experienced two deaths, and the emotion was too much to bear. The sun shined brightly through the window, blinding me. I let out a huge sigh and moved tissues away from my cheeks. While I didn't feel completely better, I felt more at peace. It was as if my heart beat steadily with the heart of heaven. It is on those silent nights where no one could comprehend how your heart feels. It is then that your tears in the night leave a mark on your pillow, mascara stains on the spot you lay your head. While no one would ever know the thoughts that crossed your beautiful mind, it was God who knew them and sat beside you. God's word says while weeping may endure for the night, joy comes in the morning. It may seem as if the word joy is much to promise, but when you awaken from a mourning night, there is something different as you awake. Be encouraged and embrace those mascara stained pillows. Tears' running down your face brings about such healing. This life may be difficult but it can also be so great! Your tears are not in vain. Those stains on the pillow are signs that healing took place and you are human. While your duty is never done, and while you may not have it all together, you are just being real. When others tell you to be strong, it is in those tears where you will find strength again. For even Jesus weeps with His children, even He weeps with you.

Weeping may endure for a night, but joy comes in the morning.

-Psalm 30:5

Today's Prayer:

Lord,

In all weeping I may do, bring me joy and peace. Thank you for the gift of tears as they bring healing heart. Even when I know I should be strong help me find strength in you. Also remind me daily that in my weakness will be your strength. As I cry tears of sadness, may I feel your precious arms around me. When I cry tears of joy, may your presence overwhelm me.

Amen

Today's Reflections:

_____

_____

_____

_____

_____

_____

_____

_____

_____

_____

_____

_____

_____

_____

_____

_____

_____

_____

_____

_____

_____

_____

*CONSIDER IT PURE JOY
WHEN YOU FACE TRIALS
BECAUSE THE TESTING OF
YOUR FAITH PRODUCES
PERSEVERANCE!*

-James 1:2-4

DAY 39
LOADED
As I Unload My Concerns And Troubles, God Will Cleanse

While I was doing laundry one day, I saw my officer's uniform shirt. It brought back memories I will never forget. Years ago I remembered a time when he was going through what many of our officer's face day after day. Countless calls and dealing with what many of us would never want to. I remember wishing I could take it all away. I wanted to shield his eyes from people in pain, from the sight of bruised and beaten women, from the sound of crying children, or the screams of someone who just lost a loved one. I longed for the bravery he held for split second decisions he must make on the beat. There was a longing in my heart for him to have peace. If only for one second he didn't have a gathering of images in his head that no mind could bear. I didn't want my officer to hear the blood curdling sounds we could never hear without tears of our own.

As wives we can wash dirt stains from a struggle, spit from someone showing disrespect, a blood stained uniform, but we can't wash away the calls they go out to. What we wish we could take away from our officer because we love them, only God can truly carry and cleanse. As you wash your officer's uniform, remember, there are things that can't be washed away after a day on the beat. There will also be things in life we would want to see washed away, but they cannot be. Guilt and shame may drown us, regrets from our past, shame from horrible decisions, and even traumatizing images that haunt our minds. But there is a God who will take the load from you. Countless things of this world could never be washed away. Even the greatest of sins cannot be gone without a great sacrifice. We are reminded in Psalms that only God can cleanse and wash away physically and spiritually. It will take an instant of surrender on our part to see revelation. When we surrender to God, we will find our freedom and healing from the things of the world. But first we must seek a clean heart that can only be found in Him.

Wash me thoroughly from my iniquity And cleanse me from my sin.

-Psalm 51:2

Today's Prayer:

Lord,

Create in me a clean heart. With all the things my officer sees, cover him with your grace and peace to see goodness besides the chaos. I ask that you forgive me of my sins and cleanse me from all unrighteousness. Wash me white as snow. As I unload all my troubles and worries, it is you I find comfort in. Help me to surrender all things to you, so I may see your treasures revealed in my life.

Amen

Today's Reflections:

_____

_____

_____

_____

_____

_____

_____

_____

_____

_____

_____

_____

_____

_____

_____

_____

_____

_____

_____

_____

_____

_____

_____

THE HEART OF A WIFE ON DUTY IS WILLING AND COURAGEOUS! FOR NOT JUST ANYONE COULD SACRIFICE THE ONE THEIR HEART LOVES AND SEND THEM OUT INTO THE DARKNESS OF THE WORLD.

DAY 40
AT THE END OF THE SHIFT
The End Is Not Final, For The End Is Just The Beginning

Resignation. A word that brings shock, excitement, and sometimes sadness. When we hear this word we often know it means an end. We are told that when a door closes, another one opens. There will be times when we close the doors and times when the door is closed on us.

It was a year that brought many changes. We moved homes, our place of worship, said goodbye to familiar friends, and God was still calling us out. I had been a police chaplain for 5 years and while it was an amazing call, I could never imagine leaving. God was telling me, it was time to go. There was a fight between God and I while I handed Him the countless reasons I should stay. In return, He gave me one reason I should go. It was obedience. As the resignation letter was written up, tears came. There was a loss in my heart and with it I felt no value. Although many tears were shed, I also got to experience Joy. Many people left my life that year, but God brought around more. I left some of the most precious things in my life behind, not because I wanted to, but out of pure obedience to God. Although it hurt, the future may hold a discovery of "why". But even if I never know why, I will understand. It's amazing to see how the call God has on our life can come to end leading us into a new call and season. When doors close, we often seek to reopen them. When we look back we forget to turn around and see the new thing God is doing. We pray for God to prosper us and to give us hope, but fail to see His works when it seems as if our prayers are not being answered the way we see fit. Only God sees the future and knows the plan. His plans are not to cause harm, but to bring hope and to give you a future like no other because of the value you hold in the kingdom. So even if it feels like the end of the shift for you, the end is not final, it is just the beginning.

"For I know the plans I have for you," declares the Lord, "plans to prosper you and not to harm you, plans to give you hope and a future.

- Jeremiah 29:11

Today's Prayer:

Lord,

For every closed door, open my eyes to the newness. Continuously take me into new paths and directions so I may fulfill my God given destiny. Help me to be obedient to your call despite what others may think or say. Thank you for never ending the things in my life, but beginning new things in my life. Thank you for replacing what is lost. Give my family and I hope and a future in you. Close doors that need to be closed, open doors that need opening, and for the ones you open, may no man shut.

Amen

Today's Reflections:

_____

_____

_____

_____

_____

_____

_____

_____

_____

_____

_____

_____

_____

_____

_____

_____

_____

_____

_____

_____

_____

_____

To the wife on duty who woke up next to an empty pillow and to the one who will go to bed next to an empty pillow - you are not alone.

To the wife on duty who overheard people criticizing and judging his call to duty - you are not alone.

To the wife on duty who is barely hanging on - you are not alone.

To the wife on duty who had to wash blood, spit, ashes, tears, or dirt many times - you are not alone.

To the wife on duty whose heart breaks when he walks out the door - you are not alone

To the wife on duty who has to sit and watch the late breaking news and keep it together - you are not alone.

To the wife on duty who stands strong at the funeral of the fallen - you are not alone.

To the wife on duty who prays so hard with tears streaming down your face - you are not alone.

To the wife on duty who has no words to say to another wife on duty in her pain - you are not alone.

To the wife on duty who feels alone because no one could ever get this life - YOU ARE NOT ALONE!

The same God who created you, sees the strength in you. God knows every detail of your life and loves you just as you are. He loves the sound of your voice and sees your tears. He wants to take this life and all it entails so He can turn your mess into a message and into a masterpiece. So, even when you feel alone, always look to your side and remember He walks with you.

A Special Note from the Author

My marriage could have easily ended in divorce many years ago. I wanted to win the arguments, have the last word, and prove to my husband I was right and he was wrong. I wanted to ensure he knew all the wrong he did and showed it in my attitude toward him along with harsh words. I tried doing this marriage on my own and became bitter. I was so hurt like never, felt so betrayed, felt so lost until I tired of it. I knew of God but really didn't pray until I needed something. Even then, my faith wasn't really there. It took packing up bags a few times and making threats to leave that led me to a breakdown in our living room.

One afternoon, I cried out to God in the living room while my children were taking a nap. I wanted God to change my husband and fix my marriage. Did God show up? You bet he did, but he didn't want to change my husband, he wanted to change me. It didn't seem fair. As I allowed God to move in my heart and open my eyes to things I was not seeing in my marriage, God transformed so much. I then found a powerful promise in the bible that said, "If a husband is lost, he would be won over by the actions of the wife." Over time, patience, lots of learning, and determination, God saved my marriage.

Since you have journeyed through this devotional, I wanted to share this with those of you who may need help not just in life circumstances, but even in your marriage today. You may have heard of Jesus and not sure if He is someone you can trust, or you may wonder if he is the answer, but find yourself hesitant to release it all to him. Please know God knew you would hold this book right now. He wants you know He is right there with you and ready to hear your sweet voice talk to him. He wants to help you. He wants your heart. He wants to take all the hurt and pain and make all things new in your life. If you are ready to commit your life to him pray this, "God, I know I have sinned, I know I am not where I want to be, and I want your forgiveness! I believe Jesus died on the cross to pay the price for my sins. Please wash me clean from all sin, shame, and guilt. Come into my life Jesus, to be my Lord and Savior. I ask this in your name Jesus Christ, Amen."

Life will be full of challenges, but God is bigger than them and will hold your hand through it all. Stay focused on the word of God, read devotionals that will encourage you each day. Connect with those who will support you. And remember…in the morning when you rise, God has risen with you.

Prayer for a Wife on Duty

May you go in pursuit of God in every aspect of your life.

May you seek to have roll call each morning announcing you are present and ready to face the day and all it entails with God as your backup.

May the Lord cuff your heart with His, revealing all of His love and mysteries as you seek him.

May you search God with all your heart and love him with all your strength.

May the Lord help you overcome all you are facing and protect your heart.

Patrol your heart, mind, and speech arresting all that is displeasing to God and ask Him to remove it.

May you put on the full armor of God and dress yourself in spiritual righteousness, just as your officer does in the physical each day.

May you call unto God in faith he hears you, just as a call is said over a radio in faith that help is on the way.

May the Lord sustain you. May you never underestimate the passion and love God has for you. May you arrest God's word and take hold of it, capturing its strength, beauty, and watching it live out in your life.

May the Lord bless you beyond measure. May the Lord bless you precious wife on duty.

The Seven Prayers Of A Wife On Duty

1. That God would go before, behind, and beside my officer.
2. For God to give him wisdom and insight as he responds to every call
3. For the tenderness of his heart to be shielded from what his eyes see daily.
4. May the strength of the Lord guide him in his role at home and help him transition after duty to be the husband and father he is called to be.
5. For his mind to be one of peace despite the chaos he faces and for his heart to resist temptation.
6. That as I kiss him goodbye and send him off to duty, that he would know just how much I love and support him.
7. May the God of peace be the one he turns to in everything he faces, so he may know God is bigger.

ABOUT THE AUTHOR

Allison P. Uribe is founder of Wives on Duty Ministries. She is an author, chaplain, and sought after speaker. As the wife of a San Antonio, Texas Police Officer she has reached wives internationally, encouraging them in their journey as a police wife.

44619280R00140

Made in the USA
San Bernardino, CA
18 January 2017